Taste of Home's
Diabetic
Cookbook 2007

Taste of Home Books

Executive Editor, Books: Heidi Reuter Lloyd
Senior Book Editor: Mark Hagen
Associate Food Editor: Diane Werner, R.D.
Recipe Editor: Sue A. Jurack

Front cover photography by Reiman Publications.
Photographer: Rob Hagen

Pictured on the front cover: Penne with Roasted Tomato Sauce and Mozzarella *(page 102).*

Pictured on the back cover *(clockwise from top right):* Baked Bean Stew *(page 68),* Mocha Cappuccino Ice Cream Pie *(page 153)* and Broiled Caribbean Sea Bass *(page 65).*

ISBN-13: 978-1-4127-2488-3
ISBN-10: 1-4127-2488-0

ISSN: 1554-0103

Manufactured in China.

8 7 6 5 4 3 2 1

Nutritional Analysis: Every effort has been made to check the accuracy of the nutritional information that appears with each recipe. However, because numerous variables account for a wide range of values for certain foods, nutritive analyses in this book should be considered approximate. Different results may be obtained by using different nutrient databases and different brand-name products.

Microwave Cooking: Microwave ovens vary in wattage. Use the cooking times as guidelines and check for doneness before adding more time.

Preparation/Cooking Times: Preparation times are based on the approximate amount of time required to assemble the recipe before cooking, baking, chilling or serving. These times include preparation steps such as measuring, chopping and mixing. The fact that some preparations and cooking can be done simultaneously is taken into account. Preparation of optional ingredients and serving suggestions is not included.

Note: This book is for informational purposes and is not intended to provide medical advice. Neither Publications International, Ltd., nor the authors, editors or publisher takes responsibility for any possible consequences from any treatment, procedure, exercise, dietary modification, action, or applications of medication or preparation by any person reading or following the information in this cookbook. The publication of this book does not constitute the practice of medicine, and this cookbook does not attempt to replace your physician, pharmacist or other health-care provider. **Before undertaking any course of treatment or nutrition plan, the authors, editors and publisher advise the reader to check with a physician or other health-care provider.**

Not all recipes in this cookbook are appropriate for all people with diabetes. Health-care providers, registered dietitians and certified diabetes educators can help design specific meal plans tailored to individual needs.

Taste of Home's Diabetic Cookbook 2007

Personalizing Your Healthy Lifestyle

Pork and Sweet Potato Skillet (page 80)

EATING FOR LIFE...
THE DIABETIC WAY

Guess what! If you have diabetes, you no longer have to shy away from scrumptious, taste-tempting foods. Today, family cooks are serving dishes that satisfy everyone at the table—just consider the sensational recipes in this collection.

As the fourth edition in this classic series, *Taste of Home's Diabetic Cookbook 2007* is filled with delicious recipes sure to whet your appetite...whether you have diabetes or not.

Flip through the pages and you'll find everything from savory appetizers to show-stopping desserts. Need a comforting entrée that fits into a busy weeknight? This cookbook is loaded with deliciously healthy options. Useful tips are also scattered throughout, suggesting ways to streamline preparation and stay on track with healthful eating.

In addition, colorful icons help you find dishes that specifically fit your needs. These symbols denote recipes prepared within 30 minutes or less, those sized right for two people, and recipes particularly low in fat or carbohydrates, for example. (See page 7 for a complete list of icons.)

At the back of the book, you'll find two indexes—one, a standard listing of the book's recipes; and the other, recipes grouped by icons. Every recipe includes nutritional information and diabetic exchanges, making it a breeze to whip up delectable menus for the entire family.

With this edition of *Taste of Home's Diabetic Cookbook,* keeping nutrition at the forefront has never been easier...or tastier. We hope you enjoy the dishes shared here, and we're sure many of them will be requested by family and friends time and again.

Diane Werner, R.D.

MAKING THE CHANGE
It's Easier Than You Think!

By turning to this cookbook, you've already taken the first step to a healthier new you. Next, consider a divide-your-plate strategy at mealtimes. Imagine your plate separated into three sections.

• Fill one half of the plate with vegetables.

• One fourth of the plate should feature a lean protein—such as fish, chicken, turkey, lean beef or pork, beans or even tofu.

• Reserve the last portion for a whole grain or starchy side dish such as brown rice, whole wheat pasta, small baked potato or whole grain bread.

SETTING A TIMETABLE

Eating at regular intervals helps keep blood glucose levels fairly consistent. If you're like most people, however, you know that keeping a schedule isn't easy. Occasionally straying from an eating schedule is all right as long as the rest of your day is planned accordingly.

If you're in a situation that requires you to eat earlier than usual, for example, skip a carbohydrate serving and have it at your regular mealtime. When eating later than you're used to, have a carbohydrate serving or your evening snack during your traditional mealtime to tide you over until you can enjoy a complete menu.

When you're on the go and absolutely need to eat something, fast-food is an option when nothing else is available. Just be sure to order small sizes, avoid deep-fried and breaded items, and omit oily dressings and mayonnaise-based sauces.

Consider any one of the following options the next time you're at the drive-thru:

• Plain, kid-sized hamburger
• Small baked potato with minimal toppings
• Cup of chili or noodle/vegetable soup
• Fruit and yogurt parfait
• Basic taco
• Plain, soft pretzel
• Half of a turkey or roast beef sandwich
• Slice of thin-crust cheese pizza

SATISFYING A SNACK ATTACK

There's more great news for people with diabetes! Treats are no longer off-limits as long as you control the type and amount of snack in which you indulge.

Here's a savory specialty that curbs temptation when the munchies come calling, as well as two recipes that satiate the sweet tooth. Best of all, these treats are perfect for the whole family.

Spiced Honey Pretzels

4 cups thin pretzel sticks
3 tablespoons honey
2 teaspoons butter or stick margarine, melted
1 teaspoon onion powder
1 teaspoon chili powder

Preheat oven to 350°F. Line 15x10x1-inch baking pan with foil; coat foil with nonstick cooking spray. Place pretzels in large bowl. Combine honey, butter, onion powder and chili powder in small bowl. Pour over pretzels; toss to coat evenly. Spread into prepared pan. Bake at 350(o)F for 8 minutes, stirring once. Cool on wire rack, stirring gently several times to separate.

Makes 8 servings

Nutrients per Serving: 1/2 cup

Calories 98	**Fiber** 1g
Fat 1g (sat 1g)	**Cholesterol** 3mg
Protein 2g	**Sodium** 487mg
Carbohydrate 20g	

Exchanges: 1-1/2 starch

Pudding Grahamwiches

1-1/2 cups cold fat-free milk
1 package (1 ounce) sugar-free instant vanilla pudding mix
1 carton (8 ounces) frozen reduced-fat whipped topping, thawed
1 cup miniature marshmallows
24 graham crackers (about 5x2-1/2 inches each), broken in half
5 tablespoons miniature semisweet chocolate chips

Whisk milk and pudding mix in large bowl for 2 minutes. Let stand 2 minutes or until soft-set. Fold in whipped topping and marshmallows. Spread pudding mixture over half of graham crackers. Top with remaining crackers. Place chocolate chips in shallow dish. Press edges of sandwiches into chips to coat. Wrap each sandwich in plastic wrap; place in airtight container and freeze. Remove from freezer about 5 minutes before serving.

Makes 2 dozen servings

Nutrients per Serving: 1 sandwich

Calories 108	**Fiber** 1g
Fat 3g (sat 2g)	**Cholesterol** <1mg
Protein 2g	**Sodium** 143mg
Carbohydrate 18g	

Exchanges: 1 starch, 1/2 fat

Mini Rice Cake Snacks

3 ounces reduced-fat cream cheese
1/4 cup orange marmalade
24 miniature honey-nut or cinnamon-apple rice cakes
2 medium fresh strawberries, sliced
3 tablespoons fresh blueberries
3 tablespoons mandarin orange segments
3 tablespoons pineapple tidbits

Combine cream cheese and marmalade in small bowl until blended. Spread over rice cakes; top with fruit.

Makes 8 servings

Nutrients per Serving: 3 rice cake snacks

Calories 81	**Fiber** 1g
Fat 2g (sat 1g)	**Cholesterol** 6mg
Protein 2g	**Sodium** 57mg
Carbohydrate 15g	

Exchanges: 1/2 starch, 1/2 fruit

Q & A

What foods can I enjoy without guilt?

You can partake in most any food as long as you don't overindulge. Remember that the key to healthy eating is moderation. For instance, air-popped popcorn may be low in fat, but it still has calories and carbohydrates. Controlling portion sizes allows you to sample a wide variety of foods, including your favorites, while keeping your blood sugar in check.

Isn't controlling my blood sugar easier if I eat the same things every day?

While this plan may control blood glucose levels, it's not very nutritious and could become pretty boring, as well. Check your blood glucose two hours from the start of a meal and you'll eventually learn how various foods, and different combinations of foods, affect you.

Can you recommend any Web sites with timely information about diabetes and nutrition?

• National Diabetes Education Program (**www.ndep.nih.gov/diabetes/MealPlanner/**) Consider this tool when learning how to plan meals.

• Joslin Diabetes Center (**www.joslin.org/managing_your_diabetes_709. asp**) This site offers nutrition facts and other ideas to help manage diabetes.

• Light & Tasty (**www.lightandtasty.com**) The Web site for the popular healthy-cooking magazine offers plenty of free recipes—all with nutrition information.

Helpful Organizations:
• American Dietetic Association: **www.eatright.org**
• American Diabetes Association **www.diabetes.org**
• U.S. Food and Drug Administration **www.fda.gov**

MEAL-PLANNING APPROACHES– EXCHANGES/CARBOHYDRATE COUNTING

People with diabetes can choose from several meal-planning approaches. Regardless of the plan used, one principle remains a common factor—all meal plans are designed to encourage you to eat similar amounts of carbohydrate at similar times each day.

EXCHANGE LISTS AND THE EXCHANGE SYSTEM

The exchange system categorizes foods into three main groups: carbohydrates, proteins and fats. An exchange system meal plan doesn't dictate what foods you eat. Instead, you choose from "exchange lists" of foods with similar nutritional make-up. For example, foods from the carbohydrate/starch group—such as a slice of bread, a small baked potato or 3/4 cup of unsweetened dry cereal—all have about the same amount of carbohydrate, protein and fat. Therefore, they are all exchangeable with each other.

An advantage of the exchange system is that it's still the common language used for communicating about food and diabetes. Cookbooks, magazine food articles and even some food labels use it.

CARBOHYDRATE COUNTING

Carbohydrate counting is keeping track of the number of carbohydrate grams you eat each day, not the individual foods. An individualized meal plan is designed so you eat a specific number of carbohydrate grams at each meal and snack. You then choose foods that total the specified number of carbohydrates.

Carbohydrate counting is based on the fact that within one to two hours of eating, 90% to 100% of digestible starches and sugars turn up in your blood as glucose. So the amount of carbohydrate you eat may also determine the amount of medication you need to cover the rise in blood glucose from meals and snacks.

How do you know how many grams of carbohydrate are in foods? The Nutrition Facts panel on packaged foods lists the grams of carbohydrate in a serving.

Every recipe in this book lists grams of carbohydrate per serving, as well as the exchange information. An advantage of carbohydrate counting is you only keep track of carbs, instead of all components of your diet.

HOW NUTRITIONAL ANALYSES WERE CALCULATED

- When a choice of ingredients is given in a recipe (such as 1/3 cup of sour cream or plain yogurt), the first ingredient listed was the one used for calculating the Nutrients per Serving.

- Recipe or plate garnishes were not included in the calculations.

- Optional ingredients were not included in the calculations.

- When a range was given (such as 2 to 3 teaspoons), the first amount listed was used.

- Only the amount of marinade absorbed during preparation was used in the calculations.

ABOUT THE ICONS

You will find special icons included with many recipes in the book. With these, you can determine at a glance which recipes fit your needs. Here is a simple explanation of the icons:

 3 grams or less per serving

 140 milligrams or less per serving

 10 grams or less per serving

Quick Recipe: 30 minutes or less total preparation and cook time

 5 grams or more per serving

 includes eggs and dairy products

 recipe serves 1 or 2 people

Appetizers

ᴥ ᴥ ᴥ

Apricot Chicken Sandwiches

Quick Recipe   *(Pictured at left)*

6 ounces poached chicken breast tenders
2 tablespoons no-sugar-added apricot fruit spread
2 tablespoons chopped pitted fresh apricots
4 slices whole wheat bread
4 lettuce leaves

1. Drain cooked chicken; chop well. Mix with apricot spread and chopped fruit.

2. Top bread with lettuce leaves. Divide chicken mixture evenly among bread slices; slice in half, folding over to make half-sandwiches. Slice each half again to make 2 wedges. Serve immediately.   *Makes 4 servings*

Nutrients per Serving: 2 sandwich wedges

Calories 175	**Fiber** 3g
Fat 4g (sat 1g)	**Cholesterol** 17mg
Protein 10g	**Sodium** 348mg
Carbohydrate 26g	

Exchanges: 1-1/2 starch, 1 lean meat

Clockwise from top left: *Banana Freezer Pops (page 20), Super Nachos (page 18), Chicken Wrap (page 22) and Apricot Chicken Sandwiches*

Bruschetta

Quick Recipe   *(Pictured at right)*

Nonstick cooking spray
1 cup thinly sliced onion
1/2 cup chopped seeded fresh tomato
2 tablespoons capers
1/4 teaspoon black pepper
3 cloves garlic, finely chopped
1 teaspoon olive oil
4 slices French bread
1/2 cup shredded reduced-fat Monterey
   Jack cheese

1. Spray large nonstick skillet with cooking spray. Heat over medium heat until hot. Add onion; cook and stir 5 minutes. Stir in tomato, capers and pepper. Cook 3 minutes.

2. Preheat broiler. Combine garlic and olive oil in small bowl. Brush bread slices with mixture. Top with onion mixture; sprinkle with cheese. Place on baking sheet. Broil 3 minutes or until cheese melts.   *Makes 4 servings*

Nutrients per Serving: 1 bruschetta slice

Calories 90	**Fiber** <1g
Fat 2g (sat <1g)	**Cholesterol** 0mg
Protein 3g	**Sodium** 194mg
Carbohydrate 17g	

Exchanges: 1 starch, 1/2 lean meat

Spinach-Stuffed Appetizer Shells

18 jumbo pasta shells (about 6 ounces)
1 package (10 ounces) frozen chopped
   spinach, thawed and well drained
1 can (8 ounces) water chestnuts, drained
   and chopped
3/4 cup fat-free ricotta cheese
1/2 cup reduced-fat mayonnaise
1/4 cup finely chopped carrot
3 tablespoons finely chopped onion
3/4 teaspoon garlic powder
3/4 teaspoon hot pepper sauce

1. Cook shells according to package directions, omitting salt. Rinse under cold running water until shells are cool; drain well.

2. Combine remaining ingredients in medium bowl; mix well.

3. Fill each shell with about 3 tablespoons spinach mixture; cover. Refrigerate up to 12 hours before serving.   *Makes 18 servings*

Nutrients per Serving: 1 stuffed shell

Calories 78	**Fiber** 2g
Fat 3g (sat 1g)	**Cholesterol** 1mg
Protein 3g	**Sodium** 86mg
Carbohydrate 11g	

Exchanges: 1/2 starch, 1/2 vegetable, 1/2 fat

Tip

Traditionally, bruschetta is a slice of Tuscan bread, lightly roasted on an open fire, brushed with a clove of garlic, drizzled with a dash of extra-virgin olive oil and dusted with a pinch of salt. Today, besides being baked in a conventional oven, the bread generally used is a French baguette that is topped with a variety of ingredients—most frequently tomatoes, olives and cheese.

Bruschetta

Szechuan Chicken Tenders

`low carb`

Quick Recipe   *(Pictured at right)*

> 2 tablespoons reduced-sodium soy sauce
> 1 tablespoon chili sauce
> 1 tablespoon dry sherry
> 2 cloves garlic, minced
> 1/4 teaspoon red pepper flakes
> 16 chicken breast tenders (about 1 pound)
> 1 tablespoon peanut oil
> Hot cooked rice (optional)
> Thinly sliced fresh green onion (optional)

1. Combine soy sauce, chili sauce, sherry, garlic and red pepper flakes in shallow dish. Add chicken; coat well.

2. Heat oil in large nonstick skillet over medium heat until hot. Add chicken; cook 6 minutes, turning once, or until chicken is browned and no longer pink in center.

3. Serve chicken with rice sprinkled with green onion, if desired.   *Makes 4 servings*

Hint: If you can "take the heat," try adding a few Szechuan peppers to this mouthwatering dish. Heat them in the oven or over a low flame in a skillet for a few minutes before adding them.

Nutrients per Serving: 4 chicken tenders (about 3 ounces cooked weight) without rice

Calories 153	**Fiber** <1g
Fat 4g (sat 1g)	**Cholesterol** 67mg
Protein 27g	**Sodium** 421mg
Carbohydrate 3g	

Exchanges: 3 lean meat

Veggie Pitas Pizzas

`low fat` `meatless`

Quick Recipe

> 2 (4-inch) whole wheat pita bread rounds, cut in half horizontally (to make 4 rounds)
> 1/4 cup pizza sauce
> 1 teaspoon dried basil
> 1/8 teaspoon red pepper flakes (optional)
> 1/2 cup thinly sliced green bell pepper
> 1/2 cup sliced red onion
> 1 cup sliced fresh mushrooms
> 1 cup shredded part-skim mozzarella cheese
> 2 teaspoons grated Parmesan cheese

1. Preheat oven to 475°F.

2. Arrange pita rounds, rough sides up, in single layer on large nonstick baking sheet. Spread 1 tablespoon pizza sauce evenly over each round to within 1/4 inch of edge. Sprinkle with basil and red pepper flakes, if desired. Top with bell pepper, onion, mushrooms and mozzarella.

3. Bake 5 minutes or until cheese is melted and pita edges are golden brown. Remove from oven. Sprinkle 1/2 teaspoon Parmesan over each round.   *Makes 4 servings*

Nutrients per Serving: 1 pizza

Calories 113	**Fiber** 2g
Fat 2g (sat 1g)	**Cholesterol** 6mg
Protein 11g	**Sodium** 402mg
Carbohydrate 13g	

Exchanges: 1/2 starch, 1 vegetable, 1 lean meat

Szechuan Chicken Tenders

Vegetable-Topped Hummus

Vegetable-Topped Hummus

Quick Recipe   *(Pictured above)*

1 can (about 15 ounces) chickpeas, rinsed and drained
2 tablespoons tahini*
2 tablespoons lemon juice
1 clove garlic
3/4 teaspoon salt
1 fresh tomato, seeded and chopped
2 green onions, finely chopped
2 tablespoons chopped fresh parsley
    Pita bread wedges or assorted crackers (optional)

*Tahini, a thick paste made of ground sesame seeds, is used in Middle Eastern cooking.

1. Combine chickpeas, tahini, lemon juice, garlic and salt in food processor or blender container; process until smooth.

2. Combine tomato, onions and parsley in small bowl. Transfer chickpea mixture to medium serving bowl; spoon tomato mixture over top. Serve with pita bread or crackers, if desired.

Makes 8 servings

Nutrients per Serving: about 6 tablespoons
(3 tablespoons hummus plus 3 tablespoons vegetables)

Calories 82	**Fiber** 3g
Fat 3g (sat <1g)	**Cholesterol** 0mg
Protein 3g	**Sodium** 429mg
Carbohydrate 11g	

Exchanges: 1/2 starch, 1 vegetable, 1/2 fat

ぉ ぉ ぉ

Pineapple-Orange Fruit Dip

Quick Recipe

1 container (6 ounces) vanilla fat-free yogurt
2 ounces reduced-fat cream cheese
1 can (8 ounces) crushed pineapple in juice, drained
1-1/2 tablespoons sugar substitute*
1/2 teaspoon grated orange peel
1/2 teaspoon grated fresh gingerroot
1/4 teaspoon ground cinnamon
    Assorted fresh fruit (optional)

*This recipe was tested with sucralose-based sugar substitute.

1. Place all ingredients in food processor or blender container; process until very smooth.

2. Serve immediately with assorted fresh fruit, if desired, or refrigerate up to 24 hours.

Makes 8 servings

Nutrients per Serving: 2 tablespoons dip (without fruit)

Calories 57	**Fiber** <1g
Fat 1g (sat 1g)	**Cholesterol** 4mg
Protein 2g	**Sodium** 36mg
Carbohydrate 11g	

Exchanges: 1/2 fruit, 1/2 fat

Turkey-Broccoli Roll-Ups

Quick Recipe

   2 pounds fresh broccoli spears
1/3 cup fat-free sour cream
1/4 cup reduced-fat mayonnaise
   2 tablespoons orange juice concentrate
   1 tablespoon Dijon mustard
   1 teaspoon dried basil
   1 pound lean smoked turkey breast, very
      thinly sliced

Microwave Directions

1. Arrange broccoli spears in single layer in large, shallow microwave-safe dish. Add 1 tablespoon water. Cover dish tightly with plastic wrap; vent. Microwave on HIGH 6 to 7 minutes or just until broccoli is crisp-tender, rearranging spears after 4 minutes. Carefully remove plastic wrap; drain broccoli. Immediately place broccoli in cold water to stop cooking; drain well. Pat dry with paper towels.

2. Combine sour cream, mayonnaise, juice concentrate, mustard and basil in small bowl. Cut turkey slices into 2-inch-wide strips. Spread sour cream mixture evenly onto strips. Place 1 broccoli spear at short end of each strip. Starting at short end, roll up tightly, allowing broccoli spear to protrude from one end. Place on serving platter; cover with plastic wrap. Refrigerate until ready to serve.

Makes about 20 servings

Note: To blanch broccoli on stove top, bring small amount of water to a boil in saucepan. Add broccoli spears; cover. Simmer 2 to 3 minutes or until broccoli is crisp-tender. Immediately place broccoli in cold water to stop cooking; drain well. Continue as directed.

Nutrients per Serving: 2 roll-ups

Calories 51	**Fiber** 2g
Fat 1g (sat <1g)	**Cholesterol** 10mg
Protein 7g	**Sodium** 259mg
Carbohydrate 4g	

Exchanges: 1 vegetable, 1 lean meat

Pizza Rollers

Quick Recipe   *(Pictured below)*

   1 package (10 ounces) refrigerated pizza
      dough
1/2 cup pizza sauce
  18 slices turkey pepperoni
   6 sticks mozzarella string cheese (1 ounce
      each)

1. Preheat oven to 425°F. Coat baking sheet with nonstick cooking spray.

2. Roll out pizza dough on prepared baking sheet to form 12×9-inch rectangle. Cut pizza dough into 6 (4-1/2×4-inch) rectangles. Spread about 1 tablespoon sauce down center third of each rectangle. Top with 3 slices pepperoni and 1 stick of mozzarella cheese. Bring ends of dough together over cheese, pinching to seal. Place seam side down on prepared baking sheet.

3. Bake in center of oven 10 minutes or until golden brown.   *Makes 6 servings*

Nutrients per Serving: 1 Pizza Roller

Calories 222	**Fiber** 3g
Fat 9g (sat 4g)	**Cholesterol** 27mg
Protein 13g	**Sodium** 602mg
Carbohydrate 24g	

Exchanges: 1 starch, 1 vegetable, 1 lean meat, 1-1/2 fat

Pizza Rollers

Cinnamon Caramel Corn

(Pictured at right)

**8 cups air-popped popcorn (about
1/3 cup unpopped kernels)
2 tablespoons honey
4 teaspoons butter
1/4 teaspoon ground cinnamon**

1. Preheat oven to 350°F. Spray jelly-roll pan with nonstick cooking spray. Place air-popped popcorn in large bowl.

2. Stir honey, butter and cinnamon in small saucepan over low heat until butter is melted and mixture is smooth; immediately pour over popcorn. Toss with spoon to coat evenly. Pour onto prepared pan; bake 12 to 14 minutes or until coating is golden brown and appears crackled, stirring twice during baking. Let cool on pan 5 minutes. (As popcorn cools, coating becomes crisp. If not crisp enough, or if popcorn softens upon standing, return to oven and heat 5 to 8 minutes.)   *Makes 4 servings*

Cajun Popcorn: Preheat oven and prepare jelly-roll pan as directed above. Combine 7 teaspoons honey, 4 teaspoons butter and 1 teaspoon Cajun or Creole seasoning in small saucepan. Proceed with recipe as directed above. Makes 4 servings.

Italian Popcorn: Spray 8 cups of air-popped popcorn with fat-free butter-flavored spray to coat. Sprinkle with 2 tablespoons finely grated Parmesan cheese, 1/8 teaspoon black pepper and 1/2 teaspoon dried oregano. Gently toss to coat. Makes 4 servings.

Nutrients per Serving: 2 cups Cinnamon Caramel Corn

Calories 117	**Fiber** 1g
Fat 4g (sat 1g)	**Cholesterol** 0mg
Protein 2g	**Sodium** 45mg
Carbohydrate 19g	

Exchanges: 1 starch, 1 fat

Trail Mix Truffles

**1/3 cup dried apples
1/4 cup dried apricots
1/4 cup apple butter
2 tablespoons golden raisins
1 tablespoon reduced-fat peanut butter
1/2 cup reduced-fat granola
1/4 cup graham cracker crumbs, divided
1/4 cup mini chocolate chips
1 tablespoon water**

Place apples, apricots, apple butter, raisins and peanut butter in food processor container; process until smooth. Stir in granola, 1 tablespoon crumbs, chocolate chips and water. Place remaining 3 tablespoons crumbs in small bowl. Shape mixture into 16 balls; roll in remaining crumbs. Cover; refrigerate until ready to serve.
Makes 8 servings

Nutrients per Serving: 2 truffles

Calories 121	**Fiber** 2g
Fat 4g (sat 1g)	**Cholesterol** 0mg
Protein 3g	**Sodium** 14mg
Carbohydrate 20g	

Exchanges: 1 starch, 1/2 fruit, 1/2 fat

Tip

If your local grocer doesn't stock apple butter, you can easily make your own. Combine 1 (23-ounce) jar (2-1/2 cups) unsweetened applesauce, 1/2 cup unsweetened apple juice concentrate, 1 teaspoon ground cinnamon, 1/2 teaspoon salt, 1/2 teaspoon ground cloves and 1/8 teaspoon ground allspice in a medium heavy saucepan. Cook over medium heat 50 minutes or until very thick, stirring occasionally. Refrigerate in a sealed container up to 3 weeks.

*Clockwise from top left: Italian
Popcorn, Cinnamon Caramel
Corn and Cajun Popcorn*

Mushrooms Rockefeller

low fat · low sodium · low carb

(Pictured at right)

- 18 large fresh button mushrooms (about 1 pound)
- 2 slices bacon
- 1/4 cup chopped onion
- 1 package (10 ounces) frozen chopped spinach, thawed and squeezed dry
- 1 jar (2 ounces) chopped pimientos, drained
- 1 tablespoon lemon juice
- 1 teaspoon grated lemon peel
- Lemon slices (optional)

1. Preheat oven to 375°F. Lightly spray 13×9-inch baking dish with nonstick cooking spray; set aside.

2. Pull entire stem out of each mushroom cap. Cut thin slice from base of each stem; discard. Chop remaining stems.

3. Cook bacon in medium skillet over medium heat until crisp. Remove bacon with tongs to paper towel; set aside. Add mushroom stems and onion to hot drippings in skillet; cook and stir until onion is tender. Add spinach, pimientos, lemon juice and peel; mix well.

4. Stuff mushroom caps with spinach mixture. Place caps in single layer in prepared baking dish. Crumble bacon; sprinkle over spinach mixture. Bake 15 minutes or until heated through. Garnish with lemon slices. Serve immediately.   *Makes 18 servings*

Nutrients per Serving: 1 stuffed mushroom cap

Calories 17	**Fiber** 1g
Fat 1g (sat <1g)	**Cholesterol** 1mg
Protein 2g	**Sodium** 26mg
Carbohydrate 2g	

Exchanges: 1/2 vegetable

Super Nachos

meatless · cooking for 1 or 2

Quick Recipe   *(Pictured on page 8)*

- 12 large baked tortilla chips (about 1-1/2 ounces)
- 1/2 cup shredded reduced-fat Cheddar cheese
- 1/4 cup fat-free refried beans
- 2 tablespoons chunky salsa

Microwave Directions

1. Arrange chips in single layer on large microwave-safe plate. Sprinkle cheese evenly over chips.

2. Spoon 1 teaspoon beans over each chip; top with 1/2 teaspoon salsa.

3. Microwave on MEDIUM (50%) 1-1/2 minutes or until cheese is melted.   *Makes 2 servings*

Note: This recipe was tested in an 1100-watt microwave oven.

Conventional Directions: Preheat oven to 350°F. Substitute foil-covered baking sheet for microwave-safe plate. Assemble nachos on prepared baking sheet as directed above. Bake 10 to 12 minutes or until cheese is melted.

Variation: For a single serving of nachos, arrange 6 tortilla chips on microwave-safe plate; top each chip with 2 teaspoons cheese, 1 teaspoon refried beans and 1/2 teaspoon salsa. Microwave on MEDIUM (50%) 1 minute.

Nutrients per Serving: 6 nachos

Calories 176	**Fiber** 2g
Fat 5g (sat 2g)	**Cholesterol** 16mg
Protein 10g	**Sodium** 683mg
Carbohydrate 23g	

Exchanges: 1-1/2 starch, 1 lean meat

Warm Peanut-Caramel Dip

Quick Recipe   *(Pictured at right)*

1/4 cup reduced-fat peanut butter
2 tablespoons fat-free caramel ice cream topping
2 tablespoons fat-free milk
1 large apple, thinly sliced
4 large pretzel rods, broken in half

1. Combine peanut butter, caramel topping and milk in small saucepan. Heat over low heat, stirring constantly, until mixture is melted and warm.

2. Serve dip with apple and pretzel rods.

Makes 4 servings

Microwave Directions: Combine all ingredients except apple and pretzel rods in small microwave-safe dish. Microwave on MEDIUM (50%) 1 minute; stir well. Microwave 1 minute more or until mixture is melted and warm. Serve dip with apple and pretzel rods.

Nutrients per Serving: about 1-1/2 tablespoons dip with 4 to 6 apple slices and 2 pretzel halves

Calories 185	**Fiber** 2g
Fat 7g (sat 1g)	**Cholesterol** <1mg
Protein 6g	**Sodium** 274mg
Carbohydrate 27g	

Exchanges: 2 starch, 1 fat

Tip

This easy-to-make caramel dip also serves up as the perfect ending to dinners of all kinds. Use decorative skewers to dip banana slices, strawberries and other fresh fruit into this delicious sweet treat.

Banana Freezer Pops

(Pictured on page 8)

2 ripe medium bananas
1 can (6 ounces) frozen orange juice concentrate, thawed (3/4 cup)
1/4 cup water
1 tablespoon honey
1 teaspoon vanilla extract
8 (3-ounce) paper or plastic cups
8 wooden popsicle sticks

1. Peel bananas; break into chunks. Place in food processor or blender container. Add orange juice concentrate, water, honey and vanilla; process until smooth.

2. Pour banana mixture evenly into cups. Cover top of each cup with small piece of foil. Insert wooden popsicle stick through center of foil into banana mixture.

3. Place cups on tray; freeze about 3 hours or until firm. To serve, remove foil; tear off paper cups (or slide out of plastic cups).

Makes 8 servings

Peppy Purple Pops: Omit honey and vanilla. Substitute grape juice concentrate for orange juice concentrate.

Frozen Banana Shakes: Increase water to 1-1/2 cups. Prepare fruit mixture as directed. Add 4 ice cubes; process on high speed until mixture is thick and creamy. Makes 3 servings.

Nutrients per Serving: 1 Banana Freezer Pop

Calories 83	**Fiber** 1g
Fat <1g (sat <1g)	**Cholesterol** 0mg
Protein 1g	**Sodium** 1mg
Carbohydrate 20g	

Exchanges: 1-1/2 fruit

Hot or Cold Tuna Snacks

Quick Recipe

- 1 can (6 ounces) water-packed chunk light tuna, well drained
- 4 ounces reduced-fat cream cheese
- 1 tablespoon minced onion
- 1 tablespoon chopped fresh parsley
- 1/2 teaspoon dried oregano
- 1/2 teaspoon black pepper
- 18 (1/2-inch-thick) slices seedless cucumber
- 18 capers, rinsed and drained (optional)

1. Combine tuna, cream cheese, onion, parsley, oregano and pepper in medium bowl.

2. Mound about 1 tablespoon tuna mixture (enough to completely cover) over top of each cucumber slice. If serving cold, garnish with capers, if desired, and serve.

3. To serve hot, preheat oven to 500°F. Spray baking sheet with nonstick cooking spray. Place snacks on prepared baking sheet and bake about 10 minutes or until tops are puffed and brown. Remove from oven and transfer to serving plate. Garnish with capers, if desired.

Makes 6 servings

Note: Rinse capers to remove excess salt.

Nutrients per Serving: 3 snacks

Calories 83	**Fiber** <1g
Fat 5g (sat 2g)	**Cholesterol** 21mg
Protein 9g	**Sodium** 196mg
Carbohydrate 2g	

Exchanges: 1 lean meat, 1/2 fat

Chicken Wraps

(Pictured on page 8)

- 1/2 pound boneless skinless chicken thighs
- 1/2 teaspoon Chinese 5-spice powder
- 1/2 cup canned bean sprouts, rinsed and drained
- 2 tablespoons thinly sliced green onion
- 2 tablespoons sliced almonds
- 2 tablespoons reduced sodium soy sauce
- 4 teaspoons hoisin sauce
- 1 to 2 teaspoons hot chili sauce with garlic*
- 4 large romaine or iceberg lettuce leaves

*Hot chili sauce with garlic is available in the Asian foods section of most large supermarkets.

1. Preheat oven to 350°F. Place chicken thighs on baking sheet; sprinkle with 5-spice powder. Bake 20 minutes or until chicken is cooked through. When cool, dice chicken.

2. Place chicken in bowl. Add bean sprouts, green onion, almonds, soy sauce, hoisin sauce and chili sauce. Stir gently until combined. To serve, spoon 1/3 cup chicken mixture onto each lettuce leaf; roll or fold as desired.

Makes 4 servings

Nutrients per Serving: 1 wrap

Calories 114	**Fiber** 1g
Fat 5g (sat 1g)	**Cholesterol** 47mg
Protein 13g	**Sodium** 302mg
Carbohydrate 5g	

Exchanges: 1 vegetable, 1-1/2 lean meat

Tip

Also called Peking sauce, hoisin is a thick, reddish-brown sauce that is both sweet and spicy and widely used in Chinese cooking. It's a mixture of soybeans, garlic, chile peppers and various spices. It can be found in Asian markets and many large supermarkets. Hoisin will keep indefinitely if refrigerated.

Marinated Citrus Shrimp

- 1 pound (about 32) medium cooked shrimp, peeled and deveined, tails left intact
- 2 navel oranges, peeled and cut into segments
- 1 can (5-1/2 ounces) pineapple chunks in juice, drained and 1/4 cup juice reserved
- 2 green onions, sliced
- 1/2 cup orange juice
- 2 tablespoons minced fresh cilantro
- 2 tablespoons lime juice
- 2 tablespoons white wine vinegar
- 1 tablespoon olive or vegetable oil
- 1 clove garlic, minced
- 1/2 teaspoon dried basil
- 1/2 teaspoon dried tarragon
- White pepper (optional)

1. Combine shrimp, orange segments, pineapple chunks and green onions in large resealable plastic bag. Mix orange juice, cilantro, lime juice, vinegar, oil, garlic, basil, tarragon and reserved pineapple juice in medium bowl; pour over shrimp mixture, turning to coat. Season to taste with white pepper, if desired. Marinate in refrigerator 2 hours or up to 8 hours.

2. Spoon shrimp mixture onto plates.

Makes 16 servings

Nutrients per Serving: about 1/2 cup

Calories 51	**Fiber** 1g
Fat 1g (sat <1g)	**Cholesterol** 44mg
Protein 5g	**Sodium** 50mg
Carbohydrate 5g	

Exchanges: 1/2 fruit, 1/2 lean meat

Herbed Stuffed Tomatoes

Quick Recipe *(Pictured below)*

- 15 cherry tomatoes
- 1/2 cup 1% cottage cheese
- 1 tablespoon thinly sliced green onion
- 1 teaspoon chopped fresh chervil *or* 1/4 teaspoon dried chervil
- 1/2 teaspoon snipped fresh dill *or* 1/8 teaspoon dried dill weed
- 1/8 teaspoon lemon pepper

1. Cut thin slice off bottom of each tomato. Scoop out pulp with small spoon; discard pulp. Invert tomatoes onto paper towels to drain.

2. Combine cottage cheese, green onion, chervil, dill and lemon pepper in small bowl. Spoon into tomatoes. Serve at once, or cover and refrigerate up to 8 hours.

Makes 5 servings

Nutrients per Serving: 3 stuffed tomatoes

Calories 27	**Fiber** <1g
Fat <1g (sat <1g)	**Cholesterol** 1mg
Protein 3g	**Sodium** 96mg
Carbohydrate 3g	

Exchanges: 1 vegetable

Herbed Stuffed Tomatoes

Petite Pizzas

(Pictured at right)

1/2 cup warm water (110° to 115°F)
3/4 teaspoon active dry yeast
1/2 teaspoon sugar
3/4 cup bread flour*
3/4 cup whole wheat flour
1/4 teaspoon salt
1-1/2 teaspoons olive oil
Pizza Sauce (recipe follows)
1/4 cup finely chopped onion
1/4 cup finely chopped green bell pepper
2 ounces Italian turkey sausage, crumbled and cooked
2/3 cup sliced fresh mushrooms, cooked until tender
1/4 cup freshly grated Parmesan cheese
1/4 cup shredded part-skim mozzarella cheese

*You can substitute all-purpose flour for bread flour; however, bread flour works better with yeast since it contains more gluten.

1. To prepare crust, place warm water in small bowl. Sprinkle yeast and sugar on top; stir to combine. Let stand 10 minutes or until bubbly. Combine flours and salt in medium bowl. Stir in oil and yeast mixture; mix until smooth. Remove dough to lightly floured work surface. Knead 5 minutes or until dough is smooth and elastic. Place dough in medium bowl sprayed with nonstick cooking spray. Turn dough in bowl so top is coated with cooking spray; cover with clean kitchen towel. Let rise in warm place 45 minutes or until doubled in bulk. Punch down dough; place on lightly floured surface and knead 2 minutes more. Cover with same towel and let rise 20 minutes more. Roll out to 1/4-inch thickness and cut into 32 circles with 2-inch cookie cutter or biscuit cutter. Place on baking sheet sprayed with cooking spray. (Combine scraps of dough and roll out again, if necessary, to obtain 32 circles.)

2. Prepare Pizza Sauce. Place about 1/2 teaspoon sauce on each dough round. Spread sauce gently, leaving small border as crust.

3. Preheat oven to 400°F. Sprinkle onion and bell pepper over sauce. Top half of pizzas with cooked sausage and each of remaining 16 pizzas with 1 or 2 cooked mushroom slices. Sprinkle cheeses over all pizzas. Bake 10 minutes or until cheese melts. Serve immediately. (To reheat, warm pizzas in preheated 250°F oven 10 minutes.) *Makes 8 servings*

Pizza Sauce

1/2 teaspoon olive oil
1 clove garlic, minced
1 can (8 ounces) tomato sauce
1 tablespoon chopped fresh basil *or*
1 teaspoon dried basil
1/2 teaspoon dried oregano
Dash salt and black pepper (optional)

Heat oil in small saucepan over medium heat. Add garlic; cook and stir 1 minute, being careful not to brown garlic. Add tomato sauce, basil and oregano; simmer 20 minutes. Season with salt and black pepper, if desired.

Nutrients per Serving: 2 sausage pizzas and 2 mushroom pizzas

Calories 148	**Fiber** 2g
Fat 4g (sat 1g)	**Cholesterol** 9mg
Protein 7g	**Sodium** 357mg
Carbohydrate 22g	

Exchanges: 1 starch, 1/2 vegetable, 1/2 lean meat, 1/2 fat

Tip

Active dry yeast will keep 6 months past the expiration date if frozen. Place the yeast directly in the freezer in its original vacuum-sealed packaging. If opened, seal tightly in plastic wrap. You can use it at a later date without thawing.

Petite Pizzas

Caribbean Chutney Kabobs

(Pictured at right)

  20 (4-inch) bamboo skewers
1/2 medium pineapple
   1 medium red bell pepper, cored, seeded and cut into 1-inch pieces
   1 medium green bell pepper, cored, seeded and cut into 1-inch pieces
3/4 pound boneless skinless chicken breasts, cut into 1-inch pieces
1/2 cup mango chutney
   2 tablespoons orange juice or pineapple juice
   1 teaspoon vanilla extract
1/4 teaspoon ground nutmeg

1. To prevent burning, soak skewers in water at least 20 minutes before assembling kabobs.

2. Peel and core pineapple. Cut pineapple into 1-inch chunks. Alternately thread bell peppers, pineapple and chicken onto skewers. Place in shallow baking dish.

3. Combine chutney, orange juice, vanilla and nutmeg in small bowl; mix well. Pour over kabobs; cover. Refrigerate up to 4 hours.

4. Preheat broiler. Spray broiler pan with nonstick cooking spray. Place kabobs on prepared broiler pan; discard any leftover marinade. Broil kabobs 6 to 8 inches from heat 4 to 5 minutes per side or until chicken is no longer pink in center. Transfer to serving plates. *Makes 10 servings*

Nutrients per Serving: 2 kabobs

Calories 110	**Fiber** 2g
Fat 1g (sat <1g)	**Cholesterol** 21mg
Protein 8g	**Sodium** 22mg
Carbohydrate 17g	

Exchanges: 1 fruit, 1 lean meat

Cheesy Potato Skins

   2 tablespoons grated Parmesan cheese
   3 cloves garlic, finely chopped
   2 teaspoons dried rosemary
1/2 teaspoon salt
1/4 teaspoon black pepper
   4 medium baking potatoes, baked
   2 egg whites, lightly beaten
1/2 cup shredded part-skim mozzarella cheese
    Salsa (optional)

1. Preheat oven to 400°F. Coat baking sheet with nonstick cooking spray; set aside.

2. Combine Parmesan cheese, garlic, rosemary, salt and pepper in small bowl.

3. Cut potatoes lengthwise in half. Remove pulp, leaving 1/4-inch-thick shells. Cut each potato half lengthwise again into 2 wedges. Place 16 wedges on prepared baking sheet. Brush with egg whites; sprinkle with Parmesan cheese mixture. Bake 20 minutes.

4. Sprinkle with mozzarella cheese; bake until melted. Serve with salsa, if desired.
Makes 8 servings

Nutrients per Serving: 2 potato skin wedges

Calories 90	**Fiber** 2g
Fat 2g (sat 1g)	**Cholesterol** 5mg
Protein 5g	**Sodium** 215mg
Carbohydrate 14g	

Exchanges: 1 starch, 1/2 lean meat

Caribbean Chutney Kabobs

Rock 'n' Rollers

Rock 'n' Rollers

Quick Recipe   *(Pictured above)*

4 (6- to 7-inch) flour tortillas

4 ounces reduced-fat cream cheese, softened

1/3 cup reduced-sugar peach preserves

1 cup shredded fat-free Cheddar cheese

1/2 cup packed washed and stemmed fresh spinach

3 ounces deli-sliced lean oven-roasted or smoked turkey breast

1. Spread each tortilla with 1 ounce cream cheese; cover with 4 teaspoons preserves. Sprinkle with 1 tablespoon Cheddar cheese.

2. Arrange spinach and turkey over Cheddar cheese. Roll up tortillas; trim ends. Cover and refrigerate until ready to serve.

3. Cut diagonally into 1-inch pieces before serving.   *Makes 4 servings*

Sassy Salsa Rollers: Substitute salsa for peach preserves and shredded iceberg lettuce for spinach leaves.

Ham 'n' Apple Rollers: Omit peach preserves and spinach leaves. Substitute deli-sliced lean ham for turkey. Spread tortillas with reduced-fat cream cheese as directed; sprinkle with shredded fat-free Cheddar cheese. Top each tortilla with about 2 tablespoons finely chopped apple and 2 ham slices; roll up. Continue as directed.

Wedgies: Prepare Rock 'n' Rollers or any variation as directed, but do not roll up. Top with second tortilla; cut into wedges. Continue as directed.

Nutrients per Serving: about 3 Rock 'n' Rollers (1 whole tortilla roll-up, cut into 1-inch pieces)

Calories 275	**Fiber** 2g
Fat 7g (sat 4g)	**Cholesterol** 28mg
Protein 19g	**Sodium** 659mg
Carbohydrate 33g	

Exchanges: 2 starch, 2 lean meat, 1/2 fat

Watermelon Kebobs

Quick Recipe

6 ounces (1-inch cubes) fat-free turkey breast

6 ounces (1-inch cubes) reduced-fat Cheddar cheese

18 cubes (1-inch) seedless watermelon

6 (6-inch) bamboo skewers

Alternate cubes of watermelon between cubes of turkey and cheese threaded onto each skewer.   *Makes 6 servings*

Favorite recipe from **National Watermelon Promotion Board**

Nutrients per Serving: 1 kebob

Calories 143	**Fiber** <1g
Fat 10g (sat 6g)	**Cholesterol** 39mg
Protein 12g	**Sodium** 390mg
Carbohydrate 2g	

Exchanges: 2 lean meat, 1 fat

Pleasin' Peanutty Snack Mix

 meatless

(Pictured at bottom right)

4 cups whole wheat cereal squares *or*
   2 cups whole wheat and 2 cups corn
   or rice cereal squares
2 cups small pretzel twists or goldfish-
   shaped pretzels
1/2 cup dry-roasted peanuts
2 tablespoons creamy peanut butter
1 tablespoon honey
1 tablespoon apple juice or water
2 teaspoons vanilla extract
   Butter-flavored cooking spray
1/2 cup raisins, dried fruit bits or dried
   cherries (optional)

1. Preheat oven to 250°F.

2. Combine cereal, pretzels and peanuts in large bowl; set aside.

3. Combine peanut butter, honey and apple juice in 1-cup glass measure or small microwave-safe bowl. Microwave on HIGH 30 seconds or until hot. Stir in vanilla.

4. Drizzle peanut butter mixture evenly over cereal mixture; toss lightly to evenly coat. Place mixture in single layer in ungreased 15×10-inch jelly-roll pan; coat lightly with cooking spray.

5. Bake 8 minutes; stir. Continue baking 8 to 9 minutes or until golden brown. Remove from oven. Add raisins, if desired; mix lightly.

6. Spread mixture in single layer on large sheet of foil to cool. *Makes 10 servings*

Nutrients per Serving: 2/3 cup snack mix

Calories 212	**Fiber** 4g
Fat 6g (sat <1g)	**Cholesterol** 0mg
Protein 6g	**Sodium** 433mg
Carbohydrate 34g	

Exchanges: 2-1/2 starch, 1 fat

Spiced Sesame Wonton Crisps

 low fat | low sodium | meatless

Quick Recipe

20 (3-inch) wonton wrappers, cut in half
1 tablespoon water
2 teaspoons olive oil
1/2 teaspoon paprika
1/2 teaspoon ground cumin or chili powder
1/4 teaspoon dry mustard
1 tablespoon sesame seeds

1. Preheat oven to 375°F. Coat 2 large baking sheets with nonstick cooking spray.

2. Cut each halved wonton wrapper into 2 strips; place in single layer on prepared baking sheets.

3. Combine water, oil, paprika, cumin and mustard in small bowl. Brush oil mixture onto wonton strips; sprinkle evenly with sesame seeds.

4. Bake 6 to 8 minutes or until lightly browned. Remove to wire rack; cool completely. Transfer to serving plate. *Makes 8 servings*

Nutrients per Serving: 10 crisps

Calories 75	**Fiber** <1g
Fat 2g (sat <1g)	**Cholesterol** 3mg
Protein 2g	**Sodium** 116mg
Carbohydrate 12g	

Exchanges: 1 starch

Pleasin' Peanutty Snack Mix

Breads

ᥤᥥ ᥤᥥ ᥤᥥ

Whole Wheat Popovers

(Pictured at left)

1-1/4 cups whole wheat pastry flour*
1-1/4 cups 2% milk
   3 eggs
   2 tablespoons melted butter
1/4 teaspoon salt
   1 tablespoon cold butter, cut into 6 pieces

*Whole wheat pastry flour is available at natural food stores and some supermarkets. Half white flour mixed with half whole wheat may be substituted.

1. Position rack in lower third of oven. Preheat oven to 400°F. Spray popover pan with nonstick cooking spray. (If popover pan is not available, jumbo muffin pans or custard cups may be used.)

2. Place flour, milk, eggs, melted butter and salt in food processor or blender container. Process until batter is smooth and consistency of heavy cream. (Batter may also be blended in large bowl with electric mixer.) Meanwhile, place popover pan in oven for 2 minutes to preheat. Immediately place 1 piece of cold butter in each popover cup and return to oven 1 minute or until butter melts.

3. Fill each cup halfway with batter. Bake 20 minutes. *Do not open oven, or popovers may fall. Reduce oven temperature to 350°F.* Bake 20 minutes more. Remove popovers from cups; cool slightly on wire rack. Serve warm. *Makes 6 popovers*

Nutrients per Serving: 1 popover

Calories 181	**Fiber** 2g
Fat 9g (sat 5g)	**Cholesterol** 125mg
Protein 7g	**Sodium** 195mg
Carbohydrate 17g	

Exchanges: 1 starch, 1/2 lean meat, 1-1/2 fat

Clockwise from top left: *Whole Wheat Popovers, Low Fat Pumpkin Bread (page 40), Herb Biscuits (page 36) and Apricot Carrot Bread (page 42)*

31

Sun-Dried Tomato and Basil Bread

(Pictured at right)

1-1/2-Pound Loaf

- 1 cup water
- 4-1/2 teaspoons sugar
- 1-1/2 teaspoons salt
- 2 teaspoons dried basil
- 2 tablespoons olive oil
- 2 tablespoons toasted wheat germ
- 2-3/4 cups bread flour
- 1/4 cup whole wheat flour
- 1-1/2 teaspoons rapid-rise active dry yeast
- 1/4 cup oil-packed sun-dried tomatoes, drained and chopped

2-Pound Loaf

- 1-1/2 cups water
- 2 tablespoons sugar
- 2 teaspoons salt
- 1 tablespoon dried basil
- 3 tablespoons olive oil
- 3 tablespoons toasted wheat germ
- 3-1/2 cups bread flour
- 1/2 cup whole wheat flour
- 2 teaspoons rapid-rise active dry yeast
- 1/3 cup oil-packed sun-dried tomatoes, drained and chopped

Bread Machine Directions

1. Measuring carefully, place all ingredients except tomatoes in bread machine pan in order specified by owner's manual. Spoon tomatoes into 4 corners of pan; do not cover yeast. Program basic cycle and desired crust setting; press start.

2. Remove baked bread from pan; cool on wire rack. *Makes 12 or 16 servings (1 loaf)*

Nutrients per Serving: 1 slice (1/12 of 1-1/2-pound loaf or 1/16 of 2-pound loaf)

Calories 137	**Fiber** 1g
Fat 3g (sat <1g)	**Cholesterol** 0mg
Protein 5g	**Sodium** 302mg
Carbohydrate 25g	

Exchanges: 2 starch, 1/2 fat

Cherry Corn Muffins

- 1-1/4 cups all-purpose flour
- 3/4 cup yellow cornmeal
- 2/3 cup dried tart cherries
- 1/2 cup sugar
- 2 teaspoons baking powder
- 1/4 teaspoon salt
- 1 cup milk
- 1/4 cup vegetable oil
- 1 egg, lightly beaten
- 1 teaspoon vanilla extract

Combine flour, cornmeal, cherries, sugar, baking powder and salt in medium mixing bowl; mix well. Stir in milk, oil, egg and vanilla just until dry ingredients are moistened. Fill 12 paper-lined muffin cups three-fourths full with batter.

Bake in preheated 400°F oven 20 to 25 minutes or until wooden pick inserted into muffin centers comes out clean. Let cool in pan 5 minutes. Remove from pan and serve warm or at room temperature. *Makes 12 muffins*

Favorite recipe from **Cherry Marketing Institute**

Nutrients per Serving: 1 muffin (made with 2% milk)

Calories 199	**Fiber** 1g
Fat 6g (sat 1g)	**Cholesterol** 19mg
Protein 4g	**Sodium** 130mg
Carbohydrate 33g	

Exchanges: 1-1/2 starch, 1/2 fruit, 1 fat

Tip

Reap the health benefits of wheat germ while adding flavor and crunch to virtually any recipe. Try substituting wheat germ for the bread crumbs in meatballs, sprinkle it over the top of casseroles, or use it to coat chicken breasts.

Sun-Dried Tomato and Basil Bread

Sun-Dried Tomato Scones

Sun-Dried Tomato Scones

Quick Recipe   (Pictured above)

2 cups buttermilk baking mix
1/4 cup grated Parmesan cheese
1-1/2 teaspoons dried basil
2/3 cup 2% milk
1/2 cup oil-packed sun-dried tomatoes, drained and chopped
1/4 cup chopped green onions

1. Preheat oven to 450°F. Lightly coat baking sheet with nonstick cooking spray; set aside.

2. Combine baking mix, cheese and basil in medium bowl. Stir in milk, tomatoes and onions. Mix just until dry ingredients are moistened.

3. Drop dough by heaping teaspoonfuls onto prepared baking sheet. Bake 8 to 10 minutes or until light golden brown. Remove baking sheet to wire rack; let stand 5 minutes. Remove scones and serve warm or at room temperature.
Makes 1-1/2 dozen scones

Nutrients per Serving: 2 scones

Calories 142	**Fiber** 1g
Fat 6g (sat 2g)	**Cholesterol** 4mg
Protein 4g	**Sodium** 394mg
Carbohydrate 20g	

Exchanges: 1 starch, 1 vegetable, 1 fat

Beer Batter Rye Bread

low fat

2 cups all-purpose flour, divided
1/2 cup rye flour
2 tablespoons molasses or packed brown sugar
2 tablespoons canola oil
1 tablespoon caraway seeds
1 package (1/4 ounce) active dry yeast
1 teaspoon salt
1 cup light beer

1. Fit food processor with steel blade. Place 1 cup all-purpose flour, rye flour, molasses, oil, caraway seeds, yeast and salt in work bowl. Process about 5 seconds or until mixed.

2. Heat beer in small saucepan over low heat until temperature reaches 120° to 130°F. Turn on processor and add beer all at once through feed tube. Process about 30 seconds or until blended. Turn on processor and add remaining 1 cup flour, 1/4 cup at a time, through feed tube. Process 5 to 10 seconds after each addition. (If food processor sounds strained and/or motor slows down or stops, turn off processor immediately and stir any remaining flour into batter by hand.)

3. Coat 1-1/2-quart baking dish with nonstick cooking spray. Transfer batter from food processor container to prepared baking dish. Let stand in warm place (85°F) about 45 minutes or until almost doubled in bulk.

4. Preheat oven to 350°F. Bake loaf about 30 minutes or until wooden toothpick inserted into center comes out clean. Cool 10 minutes. Remove bread from baking dish; cool on wire rack.   *Makes 12 servings (1 loaf)*

Nutrients per Serving: 1 slice

Calories 132	**Fiber** 1g
Fat 3g (sat <1g)	**Cholesterol** 0mg
Protein 3g	**Sodium** 199mg
Carbohydrate 23g	

Exchanges: 1-1/2 starch, 1/2 fat

Smoked Focaccia

(Pictured at bottom right)

2 teaspoons sugar
1-1/2 teaspoons active dry yeast
3/4 cup warm water (110° to 115°F)
2 tablespoons finely chopped sun-dried
tomatoes, not packed in oil
1 tablespoon minced fresh basil *or*
1 teaspoon dried basil
1 tablespoon olive oil
1/2 teaspoon minced garlic
1/4 teaspoon salt
1-3/4 cups bread flour
1/4 cup cornmeal
Nonstick cooking spray
1 Grilled Bell Pepper (recipe follows)
1/4 teaspoon coarse salt

1. Sprinkle sugar and yeast over warm water; stir until yeast is dissolved. Let stand 5 to 10 minutes or until bubbly. Stir in tomatoes, basil, oil, garlic and salt. Add flour, 1/2 cup at a time, stirring until dough begins to pull away from side of bowl and forms a ball; stir in cornmeal.

2. Turn dough out onto lightly floured surface; flatten slightly. Knead gently about 5 minutes or until smooth and elastic, adding additional flour to prevent sticking, if necessary. Place dough in large bowl sprayed with nonstick cooking spray. Turn dough in bowl so all sides are coated. Let rise, covered, in warm place about 1 hour or until doubled in bulk. (Dough may be refrigerated overnight.) Prepare Grilled Bell Pepper.

3. Punch down dough; turn onto lightly floured surface and knead 1 minute. Divide dough in half; press each half into a 9×7-inch rectangle on large sheet of foil sprayed with cooking spray. Fold edges of foil to form "pan." Dimple surfaces of dough using fingertips; spray tops with cooking spray. Cut bell pepper into strips and arrange on focaccia; sprinkle with coarse salt. Let rise, covered, 30 minutes.

4. Grill focaccia (still on foil "pans") on covered grill over medium coals 8 to 12 minutes or until focaccia sound hollow when tapped. Check bottoms of focaccia after about 6 minutes; move to upper grill rack or over indirect heat to finish if browning too quickly. Cut each focaccia loaf into 3 pieces before serving (6 pieces total).

Makes 6 servings

Grilled Bell Pepper

1 large bell pepper (any color), cored,
seeded and halved lengthwise

Grill bell pepper halves, skin side down, on covered grill over medium to hot coals 15 to 25 minutes or until skin is charred, without turning. Remove from grill; cover about 10 minutes or until cool enough to handle. Remove skin with paring knife; discard.

Nutrients per Serving: 1 piece focaccia

Calories 178	**Fiber** 2g
Fat 2g (sat <1g)	**Cholesterol** 0mg
Protein 6g	**Sodium** 219mg
Carbohydrate 35g	

Exchanges: 2 starch, 1 vegetable

Smoked Focaccia

Blueberry Muffins with a Twist of Lemon

low fat

Quick Recipe   *(Pictured at right)*

> 1 cup all-purpose flour
> 1 cup uncooked old-fashioned oats
> 1/4 cup packed brown sugar
> 1 teaspoon baking powder
> 1 teaspoon baking soda
> 3/4 teaspoon ground cinnamon, divided
> 1/4 teaspoon salt
> 8 ounces lemon fat-free yogurt
> 1/4 cup egg substitute *or* 2 egg whites
> 1 tablespoon canola oil
> 1 teaspoon grated lemon peel
> 1 teaspoon vanilla extract
> 1 cup fresh or frozen blueberries
> 1 tablespoon granulated sugar
> 1 tablespoon sliced almonds (optional)

1. Preheat oven to 400°F. Spray 11 standard (2-1/2-inch) muffin cups with nonstick cooking spray; set aside.

2. Combine flour, oats, brown sugar, baking powder, baking soda, 1/2 teaspoon cinnamon and salt in large bowl.

3. Combine yogurt, egg substitute, oil, lemon peel and vanilla in small bowl; stir into flour mixture just until blended. Gently stir in blueberries. Spoon mixture into prepared muffin cups.

4. Mix granulated sugar, almonds, if desired, and remaining 1/4 teaspoon cinnamon in small bowl. Sprinkle over batter.

5. Bake 18 to 20 minutes or until lightly browned and wooden toothpick inserted into centers comes out clean. Cool slightly before serving.   *Makes 11 servings*

Nutrients per Serving: 1 muffin

Calories 136	**Fiber** 1g
Fat 2g (sat 0g)	**Cholesterol** 1mg
Protein 3g	**Sodium** 216mg
Carbohydrate 26g	

Exchanges: 1-1/2 starch

Herb Biscuits

Quick Recipe   *(Pictured on page 30)*

> 1/4 cup hot water (130°F)
> 1-1/2 teaspoons quick-rise active dry yeast
> 2-1/2 cups all-purpose flour
> 3 tablespoons sugar
> 1-1/2 teaspoons baking powder
> 1/2 teaspoon baking soda
> 1/2 teaspoon salt
> 5 tablespoons cold margarine, cut into pieces
> 2 teaspoons finely chopped fresh parsley *or* 1/2 teaspoon dried parsley flakes
> 2 teaspoons finely chopped fresh basil *or* 1/2 teaspoon dried basil
> 2 teaspoons finely chopped fresh chives *or* 1/2 teaspoon dried chives
> 3/4 cup buttermilk

1. Preheat oven to 425°F. Spray cookie sheet with nonstick cooking spray; set aside.

2. Combine hot water and yeast in small cup; let stand 2 to 3 minutes. Combine flour, sugar, baking powder, baking soda and salt in medium bowl; cut in margarine using pastry blender or 2 knives until mixture resembles coarse crumbs. Mix in parsley, basil and chives. Stir in buttermilk and yeast mixture to make soft dough. Turn dough out onto lightly floured surface. Knead 15 to 20 times.

3. Roll to 1/2-inch thickness. Cut hearts or other shapes with 2-1/2-inch cookie cutter. Place biscuits on prepared cookie sheet. Bake 12 to 15 minutes or until browned. Cool on wire racks. Serve immediately.   *Makes 18 servings*

Nutrients per Serving: 1 biscuit

Calories 156	**Fiber** 1g
Fat 5g (sat 1g)	**Cholesterol** 0mg
Protein 3g	**Sodium** 254mg
Carbohydrate 24g	

Exchanges: 1-1/2 starch, 1 fat

Blueberry Muffins with a Twist of Lemon

Orchard Fruit Bread

(Pictured at right)

3 cups all-purpose flour or oat flour blend
2/3 cup sugar
1 teaspoon baking soda
2 eggs, beaten
1 carton (8 ounces) lemon lowfat yogurt
1/3 cup vegetable oil
1 teaspoon grated lemon peel
1 can (15 ounces) DEL MONTE® LITE®
Fruit Cocktail, drained
1/2 cup chopped walnuts or pecans

1. Preheat oven to 350°F. Combine flour, sugar and baking soda; mix well.

2. Blend eggs with yogurt, oil and lemon peel. Add dry ingredients along with fruit cocktail and nuts; stir just enough to blend. Spoon into greased 9×5-inch loaf pan.

3. Bake 60 to 70 minutes or until wooden pick inserted into center comes out clean. Let stand in pan 10 minutes. Turn out onto wire rack; cool completely.   *Makes 1 loaf*

Nutrients per Serving: 1 slice (1/16 of loaf)

Calories 215	**Fiber** 1g
Fat 8g (sat 1g)	**Cholesterol** 27mg
Protein 5g	**Sodium** 98mg
Carbohydrate 32g	

Exchanges: 1-1/2 starch, 1/2 fruit, 1-1/2 fat

Tip

Change the flavor of this bread with the seasons by switching the flavor of yogurt. Try lime in the summer, banana in the spring or vanilla in the winter. You can also add raisins or use seeds in place of the nuts, such as toasted pumpkin seeds during autumn months.

Pizza Breadsticks

1 cup water
1 tablespoon olive oil
1 teaspoon salt
3 cups all-purpose flour
1/2 cup shredded mozzarella cheese
1/4 cup shredded Parmesan cheese
1/4 cup chopped red bell pepper
1 green onion, sliced
1 clove garlic, minced
1/2 teaspoon dried basil
1/2 teaspoon dried oregano
1/4 teaspoon red pepper flakes (optional)
1-1/2 teaspoons active dry yeast

Bread Machine Directions

1. Measuring carefully, place all ingredients in bread machine pan in order specified by owner's manual. Program dough cycle setting; press start. Coat large baking sheets with nonstick cooking spray; set aside.

2. When cycle is complete, remove dough to lightly floured surface. If necessary, knead in additional flour to make dough easy to handle. Roll dough into 14×8-inch rectangle. Let dough rest 5 minutes. Cut dough widthwise into 28 (8×1/2-inch) strips. Twist each strip 3 to 4 times; place 2 inches apart on prepared baking sheets, pressing both ends of each dough strip to baking sheet. Cover with clean kitchen towels; let rise in warm, draft-free place 30 minutes or until doubled in size.

3. Preheat oven to 425°F. Bake 15 to 20 minutes or until golden brown. Remove from baking sheets; cool on wire racks.

Makes 28 breadsticks

Nutrients per Serving: 1 breadstick

Calories 65	**Fiber** <1g
Fat 1g (sat 1g)	**Cholesterol** 2mg
Protein 2g	**Sodium** 99mg
Carbohydrate 11g	

Exchanges: 1 starch

Jalapeño Corn Muffins

Quick Recipe

MAZOLA NO STICK® Cooking Spray
1 cup flour
1 cup yellow corn meal
2 teaspoons baking powder
1/4 teaspoon salt
2 eggs
1/2 cup KARO® Light Corn Syrup
1/4 cup MAZOLA® Oil
1 cup cream-style corn
1 cup (4 ounces) shredded Monterey Jack cheese
2 tablespoons chopped, seeded jalapeño peppers, fresh or pickled*

*Jalapeño peppers can sting and irritate the skin, so wear rubber gloves when handling peppers and do not touch your eyes.

1. Preheat oven to 400°F. Spray 12 (2-1/2-inch) muffin pan cups with cooking spray.

2. In medium bowl combine flour, corn meal, baking powder and salt.

3. In large bowl combine eggs, corn syrup and oil. Stir in flour mixture until well blended. Stir in corn, cheese and peppers. Spoon into prepared muffin pan cups.

4. Bake 15 to 20 minutes or until lightly browned and firm to touch. Cool in pan on wire rack 5 minutes; remove from pan.

Makes 12 muffins

Nutrients per Serving: 1 muffin

Calories 230	**Fiber** 1g
Fat 9g (sat 3g)	**Cholesterol** 44mg
Protein 6g	**Sodium** 279mg
Carbohydrate 34g	

Exchanges: 2 starch, 1/2 lean meat, 1 fat

Low Fat Pumpkin Bread

low fat · low sodium

(Pictured on page 30)

1 cup Dried Plum Purée (recipe follows) or prepared dried plum butter
1 cup granulated sugar
1 cup packed brown sugar
1 cup egg substitute
1 cup canned solid pack pumpkin
2-2/3 cups all-purpose flour
2 teaspoons baking powder
1 teaspoon baking soda
1 teaspoon ground cinnamon
1/2 teaspoon salt
1/2 teaspoon ground cloves
1/4 teaspoon ground ginger
1/4 teaspoon ground nutmeg

Preheat oven to 350°F. Coat two 8-1/2×4-1/2×2-3/4-inch loaf pans with vegetable cooking spray. In mixer bowl, beat Dried Plum Purée with sugars until well blended. Beat in egg substitute and pumpkin just until blended. In medium bowl, combine flour, baking powder, baking soda, cinnamon, salt, cloves, ginger and nutmeg; stir into dried plum purée mixture until well blended. Spoon batter into prepared pans, dividing equally. Bake in center of oven 1 hour until pick inserted into centers comes out clean. Cool in pans 10 minutes; remove from pans to wire racks to cool completely. Serve with fat-free cream cheese, if desired.

Makes 2 loaves (16 slices per loaf)

Dried Plum Purée: Combine 1-1/3 cups (8 ounces) pitted dried plums and 6 tablespoons hot water in container of food processor or blender. Pulse on and off until dried plums are finely chopped and smooth. Store leftovers in a covered container in the refrigerator for up to two months. Makes 1 cup.

Favorite recipe from **California Dried Plum Board**

Nutrients per Serving: 1 slice

Calories 110	**Fiber** 1g
Fat <1g (sat <1g)	**Cholesterol** 0mg
Protein 2g	**Sodium** 124mg
Carbohydrate 26g	

Exchanges: 1-1/2 starch

Molasses Brown Bread

(Pictured at bottom right)

1 cup all-purpose flour
1 cup graham or rye flour
1 cup whole wheat flour
1 teaspoon baking soda
1/2 teaspoon salt
1 cup buttermilk
1 cup light molasses
1/2 cup golden or dark raisins
1/2 cup chopped walnuts or pecans
Reduced-fat or fat-free cream cheese (optional)

1. Preheat oven to 350°F. Spray 9×5-inch loaf pan with nonstick cooking spray; set aside.

2. Combine all-purpose flour, graham flour, whole wheat flour, baking soda and salt in large bowl. Add buttermilk and molasses; mix well. Stir in raisins and nuts.

3. Spoon batter evenly into prepared pan. Bake 50 to 55 minutes or until wooden toothpick inserted near center comes out clean.

4. Remove pan to wire rack; let stand 10 minutes. Turn bread out onto wire rack; cool completely. Serve at room temperature with cream cheese, if desired.   *Makes about 16 servings (1 loaf)*

Nutrients per Serving: 1 slice

Calories 188	**Fiber** 3g
Fat 3g (sat <1g)	**Cholesterol** 1mg
Protein 4g	**Sodium** 177mg
Carbohydrate 37g	

Exchanges: 2 starch, 1/2 fruit, 1/2 fat

Tip

Light molasses comes from the first boiling of the sugar. Recipes made with light molasses have a subtle flavor and are lighter in color. Cookies are slightly softer, while breads are more crusty.

Banana Bread

2-1/2 cups all-purpose flour
2 teaspoons baking powder
1 teaspoon baking soda
1/2 teaspoon ground allspice
4 ripe medium bananas, mashed (2 cups)
1 cup sugar
1/2 cup MOTT'S® Natural Apple Sauce
3 egg whites
2 tablespoons vegetable oil
1 teaspoon vanilla extract

1. Preheat oven to 375°F. Spray 8×4-inch loaf pan with nonstick cooking spray.

2. In large bowl, combine flour, baking powder, baking soda and allspice.

3. In medium bowl, whisk together bananas, sugar, apple sauce, egg whites, oil and vanilla.

4. Stir apple sauce mixture into flour mixture just until moistened. Spread batter into prepared pan. Bake 60 minutes or until toothpick inserted into center comes out clean. Cool in pan 10 minutes. Invert onto wire rack; turn right side up. Cool completely. Cut into 16 slices.
Makes 16 servings (1 loaf)

Nutrients per Serving: 1 slice

Calories 167	**Fiber** 1g
Fat 2g (sat <1g)	**Cholesterol** 0mg
Protein 3g	**Sodium** 140mg
Carbohydrate 35g	

Exchanges: 2 starch, 1/2 fruit

Molasses Brown Bread

Cheesy Ham and Pepper Muffins

(Pictured at right)

2-1/2 cups all-purpose flour
3 tablespoons sugar
1 tablespoon baking powder
1/4 teaspoon black pepper
1 cup fat-free milk
6 tablespoons canola oil
2 eggs, beaten
2 tablespoons Dijon mustard
3/4 cup shredded reduced-fat Swiss cheese
3/4 cup diced cooked lean ham
3 tablespoons chopped red or green bell pepper

1. Preheat oven to 400°F. Spray 12 standard (2-1/2-inch) muffin cups with nonstick cooking spray or line with paper baking cups; set aside.

2. Combine flour, sugar, baking powder and black pepper in large bowl. Whisk together milk, oil, eggs and mustard in small bowl until blended. Stir into flour mixture just until moistened. Fold in cheese, ham and bell pepper. Spoon evenly into prepared muffin cups.

3. Bake 19 to 21 minutes or until wooden toothpick inserted into centers comes out clean. Cool in muffin pan on wire rack 5 minutes. Remove from pan and cool on wire rack 10 minutes.   *Makes 12 muffins*

Variation: You can vary the taste of these muffins by substituting 3/4 cup either shredded reduced-fat Monterey Jack cheese with jalapeños or reduced-fat Cheddar cheese for the Swiss cheese.

Nutrients per Serving: 1 muffin

Calories 230	**Fiber** 1g
Fat 10g (sat 2g)	**Cholesterol** 47mg
Protein 10g	**Sodium** 202mg
Carbohydrate 25g	

Exchanges: 1-1/2 starch, 1 lean meat, 1-1/2 fat

Apricot Carrot Bread

(Pictured on page 30)

1-3/4 cups all-purpose flour
1 teaspoon baking powder
1/4 teaspoon baking soda
1/4 teaspoon salt
1/2 cup granulated sugar
1/2 cup finely shredded carrots
1/2 cup MOTT'S® Natural Apple Sauce
1 egg, beaten lightly
2 tablespoons vegetable oil
1/3 cup dried apricots, snipped into small bits
1/2 cup powdered sugar
2 teaspoons MOTT'S® Apple Juice

1. Preheat oven to 350°F. Spray 8×4-inch loaf pan with nonstick cooking spray.

2. In large bowl, combine flour, baking powder, baking soda and salt.

3. In small bowl, combine granulated sugar, carrots, apple sauce, egg and oil.

4. Stir apple sauce mixture into flour mixture just until moistened. (Batter will be thick.) Fold in apricots. Spread batter in prepared pan.

5. Bake 45 to 50 minutes or until toothpick inserted into center comes out clean. Cool in pan 10 minutes. Invert onto wire rack; turn right side up. Cool completely. For best flavor, wrap loaf in plastic wrap or foil; store at room temperature overnight.

6. Just before serving, in small bowl, combine powdered sugar and apple juice until smooth. Drizzle over top of loaf. Cut into 12 slices.

Makes 12 servings

Nutrients per Serving: 1 slice

Calories 163	**Fiber** 1g
Fat 3g (sat <1g)	**Cholesterol** 18mg
Protein 3g	**Sodium** 119mg
Carbohydrate 32g	

Exchanges: 2 starch, 1/2 fat

Cheesy Ham and Pepper Muffins

Spice-Prune Loaf

(Pictured at right)

1 cup chopped pitted prunes

1/2 cup prune juice

1 cup all-purpose flour

1 cup whole wheat flour

1 teaspoon baking powder

3/4 teaspoon ground cinnamon

1/2 teaspoon baking soda

1/4 teaspoon ground ginger

1/8 teaspoon salt

2 egg whites

1/3 cup molasses

3 tablespoons canola oil

1/4 teaspoon vanilla extract

1. Preheat oven to 350°F. Spray 8×4-inch loaf pan with nonstick cooking spray; set aside. Combine prunes and prune juice in small saucepan. Bring to a boil over medium-high heat. Remove from heat; let stand 5 minutes.

2. Combine all-purpose flour, whole wheat flour, baking powder, cinnamon, baking soda, ginger and salt in medium bowl. Combine egg whites, molasses, oil and vanilla in small bowl. Add to flour mixture and stir until just blended. Add prune mixture; stir until just blended.

3. Pour batter into prepared pan. Bake 55 to 60 minutes or until wooden toothpick inserted into center comes out clean. Cool in pan on wire rack 10 minutes. Turn bread out onto wire rack; cool completely. Wrap and store overnight at room temperature before slicing.

Makes 16 servings (1 loaf)

Nutrients per Serving: 1 slice

Calories 133	**Fiber** 2g
Fat 3g (sat <1g)	**Cholesterol** 0mg
Protein 3g	**Sodium** 94mg
Carbohydrate 25g	

Exchanges: 1 starch, 1/2 fruit, 1/2 fat

Wild Rice Carrot Muffins

3/4 cup all-purpose flour

3/4 cup whole wheat flour

1/2 cup packed brown sugar

2 teaspoons baking powder

1 teaspoon ground cinnamon

1/2 teaspoon salt

1/2 teaspoon ground nutmeg

2 cups well-cooked wild rice

3/4 cup skim milk

1/3 cup canola oil

1 egg, lightly beaten

1 cup grated carrots

TOPPING

1 tablespoon sugar

1/4 teaspoon ground cinnamon

Spray 12 muffin cups with nonstick cooking spray. In large bowl, combine flours, brown sugar, baking powder, 1 teaspoon cinnamon, salt and nutmeg. Add cooked wild rice; toss to coat.

In another bowl, blend milk, oil and egg; stir in carrots. Stir milk mixture into dry ingredients just enough to blend (do not overmix). Divide batter evenly among muffin cups. Combine topping ingredients; sprinkle over muffins. Bake at 400°F about 25 to 30 minutes. Remove from pan and cool. *Makes 12 servings*

Favorite recipe from **Minnesota Cultivated Wild Rice Council**

Nutrients per Serving: 1 muffin

Calories 191	**Fiber** 2g
Fat 7g (sat <1g)	**Cholesterol** 18mg
Protein 4g	**Sodium** 189mg
Carbohydrate 29g	

Exchanges: 2 starch, 1 fat

Spice-Prune Loaf

Rosemary Breadsticks

Rosemary Breadsticks

low fat

(Pictured above)

2/3 cup 2% milk
1/4 cup finely chopped fresh chives
1 teaspoon finely chopped fresh rosemary
or 1/2 teaspoon dried rosemary
3/4 teaspoon salt
1/2 teaspoon freshly ground black pepper
3/4 cup whole wheat flour
3/4 cup all-purpose flour
2 teaspoons baking powder
Nonstick cooking spray

1. Combine milk, chives, rosemary, salt and pepper in large bowl; mix well. Combine flours and baking powder in medium bowl; stir, 1/2 cup at a time, into milk mixture until blended.

2. Turn dough out onto lightly floured surface. Knead about 5 minutes or until smooth and elastic, adding more flour if sticky. Let stand 30 minutes at room temperature.

3. Preheat oven to 375°F. Spray baking sheet with cooking spray. Divide dough into 12 balls, about 1-1/4 ounces each. Roll each ball into long thin rope; place on prepared baking sheet. Lightly spray breadsticks with cooking spray. Bake about 12 minutes or until bottoms are

golden brown. Turn breadsticks over; bake about 10 minutes more or until golden brown.
Makes 12 servings

Nutrients per Serving: 1 breadstick

Calories 61	**Fiber** 1g
Fat <1g (sat <1g)	**Cholesterol** 1mg
Protein 2g	**Sodium** 220mg
Carbohydrate 12g	

Exchanges: 1 starch

✿ ✿ ✿

Peppered Cheese Baguettes

3/4 cup water
1-1/2 teaspoons salt
2 tablespoons butter, softened
1 teaspoon hot pepper sauce
2-3/4 cups all-purpose flour
1/3 cup shredded Swiss cheese
2 tablespoons grated Parmesan cheese
1/4 teaspoon black pepper
1 tablespoon sugar
2 teaspoons active dry yeast
2 tablespoons canola oil

Bread Machine Directions

1. Measuring carefully, place all ingredients except oil in bread machine pan in order specified by owner's manual. Program dough cycle setting; press start.

2. Coat 2 baking sheets with nonstick cooking spray. Divide dough into 2 equal pieces. Roll each piece into 12-inch-long rope. Place on prepared baking sheets. Cover; let rise in warm place 40 minutes or until doubled in bulk.

3. Preheat oven to 350°F. Brush dough with oil. Bake 20 to 25 minutes or until golden and loaves sound hollow when tapped. Remove bread to wire racks; cool. *Makes 12 servings (2 loaves)*

Nutrients per Serving: 1 slice (1/6 of 1 loaf)

Calories 159	**Fiber** 1g
Fat 5g (sat 2g)	**Cholesterol** 8mg
Protein 4g	**Sodium** 336mg
Carbohydrate 23g	

Exchanges: 1-1/2 starch, 1 fat

Italian Herbed Oatmeal Focaccia

2 tablespoons cornmeal
1-1/2 to 2-1/4 cups all-purpose flour, divided
1 cup QUAKER® Oats (quick or old fashioned, uncooked)
2 tablespoons dried Italian seasoning, divided
1 package (1/4 ounce, about 2-1/4 teaspoons) quick-rising yeast
2 teaspoons granulated sugar
1-1/2 teaspoons garlic salt, divided
1 cup water
1/4 cup plus 2 tablespoons olive oil, divided
4 to 6 sun-dried tomatoes packed in oil, drained and chopped
1/4 cup grated Parmesan cheese

Lightly spray 13×9-inch baking pan with no-stick cooking spray; dust with cornmeal. In large bowl, combine 1 cup flour, oats, 1 tablespoon Italian seasoning, yeast, sugar and 1 teaspoon garlic salt; mix well. In small saucepan, heat water and 1/4 cup olive oil until very warm (120°F to 130°F); stir into flour mixture. Gradually stir in enough remaining flour to make a soft dough. Turn dough out onto lightly floured surface. Knead 8 to 10 minutes or until smooth and elastic. Cover and let rest 10 minutes.

Pat dough into prepared pan, pressing dough out to edges of pan. Using fingertips, poke indentations over surface of dough. Brush remaining 2 tablespoons oil over dough. Sprinkle with remaining 1 tablespoon Italian seasoning and 1/2 teaspoon garlic salt. Arrange dried tomatoes across top; sprinkle with cheese. Cover; let rise in warm place until doubled, about 30 minutes. Heat oven to 400°F. Bake 25 to 30 minutes or until golden brown. Cut into strips or squares. Serve warm.

Makes 12 servings

Nutrients per Serving: 1 focaccia strip

Calories 163	**Fiber** 1g
Fat 8g (sat 1g)	**Cholesterol** 1mg
Protein 3g	**Sodium** 153mg
Carbohydrate 20g	

Exchanges: 1-1/2 starch, 1-1/2 fat

Lemon Walnut Muffins

3/4 cup sugar, divided
3 tablespoons finely grated lemon peel
2 tablespoons water
1 cup plain nonfat yogurt
1/2 cup skim milk
2 tablespoons vegetable oil
1 egg
2 cups all-purpose flour
1-1/4 teaspoons baking powder
1 teaspoon baking soda
1/2 teaspoon salt
3/4 cup California walnuts, chopped
1/4 cup lemon juice

Preheat oven to 375°F. Coat muffin pans with nonstick cooking spray. Combine 1/2 cup sugar, grated lemon peel and water in small saucepan. Stir over medium heat 1 to 2 minutes, just until sugar dissolves. Beat yogurt, milk, oil and egg with sugar mixture in medium bowl. Set aside.

Combine flour, baking powder, baking soda and salt in large bowl. Add sugar mixture and walnuts; stir just until batter is moistened. Do not overmix. Spoon batter into prepared muffin cups, filling each cup two-thirds full. Bake 15 to 18 minutes or until wooden toothpick inserted into center of muffins comes out clean.

Combine remaining 1/4 cup sugar and lemon juice in small bowl. Let stand 2 to 3 minutes, stirring frequently, until sugar dissolves. Remove pans from oven and pierce tops of each muffin 3 times with fork. Spoon 1 teaspoon lemon juice mixture over each muffin, letting it run over top and down edges. Cool in pan about 5 minutes before serving.

Makes 16 muffins

Favorite recipe from **Walnut Marketing Board**

Nutrients per Serving: 1 muffin

Calories 160	**Fiber** 1g
Fat 6g (sat 1g)	**Cholesterol** 14mg
Protein 4g	**Sodium** 200mg
Carbohydrate 24g	

Exchanges: 1-1/2 starch, 1 fat

Breakfast & Brunch

ৡ৹ ৡ৹ ৡ৹

Stuffed French Toast Sandwich

Quick Recipe   *(Pictured at left)*

    8 slices whole wheat or white bread
    4 slices lean deli ham (about 1 ounce each)
  3/4 cup egg substitute
  3/4 cup 2% milk
    1 tablespoon sugar
    4 tablespoons butter (optional)
    4 tablespoons reduced-sugar pancake syrup, warmed

1. Place 4 bread slices in baking pan. Top each bread slice with 1 slice of ham and another bread slice.

2. Whisk egg substitute, milk and sugar in medium bowl. Pour egg mixture over sandwiches in pan. Allow sandwiches to stand at room temperature about 5 minutes, turning once, to absorb egg mixture.

3. Spray large skillet with nonstick cooking spray; heat over medium heat. Cook sandwiches, in batches, about 2 minutes per side or until golden brown. Cut each sandwich diagonally in half and serve with 1 tablespoon butter, if desired, and syrup.   *Makes 4 servings*

Nutrients per Serving: 1 sandwich (2 halves) with 1 tablespoon syrup

Calories 275	**Fiber** 4g
Fat 7g (sat 2g)	**Cholesterol** 18mg
Protein 17g	**Sodium** 817mg
Carbohydrate 38g	

Exchanges: 2-1/2 starch, 1-1/2 lean meat

Clockwise from top left: *Eggs Benedict (page 56), Ham & Cheddar Frittata (page 56), Stuffed French Toast Sandwich and Apple & Raisin Oven Pancake (page 55)*

49

Vegetable Medley Quiche

(Pictured at right)

Nonstick cooking spray

2 cups frozen diced potatoes with onions and peppers, thawed

1 package (16 ounces) frozen mixed vegetables (such as zucchini, carrots and green beans), thawed and drained

1 can (about 10-3/4 ounces) reduced-fat condensed cream of mushroom soup, undiluted, divided

1 cup egg substitute *or* 4 eggs

1/2 cup grated Parmesan cheese, divided

1/4 cup fat-free milk

1/4 teaspoon dried dill weed

1/4 teaspoon dried thyme

1/4 teaspoon dried oregano

Dash salt and black pepper (optional)

1. Preheat oven to 400°F. Spray 9-inch pie plate with cooking spray; press potatoes onto bottom and up side of pie plate to form crust. Spray potatoes lightly with cooking spray. Bake 15 minutes.

2. Combine mixed vegetables, half of soup, egg substitute and 1/4 cup cheese in small bowl; mix well. Pour egg mixture into potato shell; sprinkle with remaining 1/4 cup cheese. *Reduce oven temperature to 375°F.* Bake 35 to 40 minutes or until set.

3. Meanwhile, combine remaining soup, milk and seasonings in small saucepan; mix well. Simmer over low heat 5 minutes or until heated through. Cut quiche into 6 wedges before serving. Serve sauce with quiche wedges.

Makes 6 servings

Nutrients per Serving: 1 wedge with about 2 tablespoons sauce

Calories 129	**Fiber** 4g
Fat 2g (sat 2g)	**Cholesterol** 5mg
Protein 9g	**Sodium** 436mg
Carbohydrate 19g	

Exchanges: 1 starch, 1 vegetable, 1 lean meat

Wild Rice Blueberry Muffins

Quick Recipe

1-1/2 cups all-purpose flour

1/2 cup sugar

2 teaspoons baking powder

1 teaspoon ground cinnamon

1/2 teaspoon salt

4 egg whites

1/2 cup skim milk

1/4 cup applesauce

1 cup fresh blueberries

1 cup well cooked, chopped wild rice

Spray nonstick cooking spray in muffin cups, or use paper liners. Preheat oven to 400°F. Combine flour, sugar, baking powder, cinnamon and salt in large bowl. Combine egg whites, milk and applesauce in separate bowl. Sprinkle 1 tablespoon dry ingredients over blueberries. Fold liquid ingredients into dry ingredients. Gently fold blueberries and wild rice into batter. Batter will be stiff. Fill prepared muffin cups two-thirds full. Bake 15 to 20 minutes or until wooden toothpick inserted into muffin centers comes out clean. *Makes 12 muffins*

Favorite recipe from **Minnesota Cultivated Wild Rice Council**

Nutrients per Serving: 1 muffin

Calories 120	**Fiber** 1g
Fat <1g (sat <1g)	**Cholesterol** <1mg
Protein 4g	**Sodium** 169mg
Carbohydrate 26g	

Exchanges: 1-1/2 starch

Cranberry Scones

Quick Recipe   *(Pictured at right)*

  1-1/2 cups all-purpose flour
    1/2 cup oat bran
    1/4 cup plus 1 tablespoon sugar, divided
      2 teaspoons baking powder
    1/2 teaspoon baking soda
    1/2 teaspoon salt
      5 tablespoons cold butter
    3/4 cup dried cranberries
    1/3 cup fat-free milk
      1 egg
    1/4 cup reduced-fat sour cream
      1 tablespoon uncooked old-fashioned or
        quick oats (optional)

1. Preheat oven to 425°F. Combine flour, oat bran, 1/4 cup sugar, baking powder, baking soda and salt in large bowl. Cut in butter with pastry blender or two knives until mixture resembles coarse crumbs. Stir in cranberries. Lightly beat milk and egg in small bowl. Reserve 2 tablespoons milk mixture. Stir sour cream into remaining milk mixture. Stir into flour mixture until soft dough forms.

2. Turn dough out onto well-floured surface. Gently knead 10 to 12 times. Shape dough into 9×6-inch rectangle. Cut dough into 6 (3-inch) squares using floured knife; cut diagonally into halves, forming 12 triangles. Place 2 inches apart on ungreased baking sheets. Brush triangles with reserved 2 tablespoons milk mixture. Sprinkle with oats, if desired, and remaining 1 tablespoon sugar.

3. Bake 10 to 12 minutes or until golden brown. Remove from baking sheets and cool on wire racks 10 minutes. Serve warm.

Makes 12 scones

Nutrients per Serving: 1 scone

Calories 168	**Fiber** 1g
Fat 6g (sat 4g)	**Cholesterol** 33mg
Protein 3g	**Sodium** 166mg
Carbohydrate 27g	

Exchanges: 1-1/2 starch, 1/2 fruit, 1 fat

Kashi® Friendly Fiber Muffins

`low fat`

      Non-stick cooking spray
      1 cup whole wheat flour
      2 teaspoons baking powder
    1/2 teaspoon salt
  1-3/4 cups KASHI® Good Friends cereal
    3/4 cup skim, rice or soy milk
      2 egg whites
    1/4 cup honey
      1 medium ripe banana, mashed
    1/4 cup unsweetened applesauce

Preheat oven to 400°F. Spray 12 (2-1/2-inch) muffin cups with cooking spray; set aside.

In small bowl, stir together flour, baking powder and salt. Set aside. In large mixing bowl, combine Kashi Good Friends cereal and milk; let stand for 2 to 3 minutes. Add egg whites and beat well. Stir in honey, banana and applesauce. Add flour mixture and mix only until dry ingredients are moistened (overmixing will produce rubbery muffins).

Divide batter among prepared muffin cups. Bake 20 to 25 minutes or until lightly browned.

Makes 12 muffins

Nutrients per Serving: 1 muffin

Calories 102	**Fiber** 2g
Fat 1g (sat <1g)	**Cholesterol** <10mg
Protein 4g	**Sodium** 210mg
Carbohydrate 22g	

Exchanges: 1-1/2 starch

Tip

It's recommended we consume 14 grams of fiber for every 1,000 calories we consume. So if you're eating 1,800 calories a day, your goal is around 25 grams of fiber. Start your day with one of these muffins, and you'll be 2 grams closer to meeting that goal!

Cranberry Scones

Sweet and Russet Potato Latkes

Quick Recipe

2 cups shredded russet potatoes
1 cup shredded sweet potato
1 cup shredded apple
3/4 cup egg substitute
1/3 cup all-purpose flour
1 teaspoon sugar
1/4 teaspoon baking powder
1/4 teaspoon salt
1/8 teaspoon ground nutmeg
Nonstick cooking spray
1 cup unsweetened cinnamon applesauce

1. Combine potatoes and apple in medium bowl. Combine egg substitute, flour, sugar, baking powder, salt and nutmeg in small bowl; add to potato mixture.

2. Spray large nonstick skillet with cooking spray; heat over medium-low heat until hot. Spoon 1 rounded tablespoonful potato mixture into skillet to form pancake about 1/4 inch thick and 3 inches in diameter.* Cook 3 minutes or until browned. Turn latke over; cook 3 minutes more or until browned. Repeat with remaining batter. Keep cooked latkes warm in preheated 250°F oven.

3. Serve latkes with applesauce.

Makes 8 servings

Three to four latkes can be cooked at one time.

Nutrients per Serving: 2 latkes with 2 tablespoons applesauce

Calories 107	**Fiber** 2g
Fat <1g (sat <1g)	**Cholesterol** 0mg
Protein 4g	**Sodium** 119mg
Carbohydrate 23g	

Exchanges: 1 starch, 1/2 fruit

Brunch Rice

Quick Recipe

1 teaspoon margarine
3/4 cup shredded carrots
3/4 cup diced green bell pepper
3/4 cup (about 3 ounces) sliced fresh mushrooms
6 egg whites, beaten
2 eggs, beaten
1/2 cup skim milk
1/2 teaspoon salt
1/4 teaspoon ground black pepper
3 cups cooked brown rice
1/2 cup (2 ounces) shredded Cheddar cheese
6 corn tortillas, warmed (optional)

Heat margarine in large skillet over medium-high heat until hot. Add carrots, bell pepper and mushrooms; cook and stir 2 minutes. Combine egg whites, eggs, milk, salt and black pepper in small bowl. Reduce heat to medium and pour egg mixture over vegetables. Continue stirring 1-1/2 to 2 minutes. Add rice and cheese; stir to gently separate grains. Heat 2 minutes. Serve immediately, or spoon mixture into warmed corn tortillas. *Makes 6 servings*

Microwave Directions: Heat margarine in 2- to 3-quart microproof baking dish. Add carrots, bell pepper and mushrooms; cover and cook on HIGH (100% power) 4 minutes. Combine egg whites, eggs, milk, salt and black pepper in small bowl; pour over vegetables. Cook on HIGH 4 minutes, stirring with fork after each minute to cut cooked eggs into small pieces. Stir in rice and cheese; cook on HIGH about 1 minute or until thoroughly heated. Serve immediately, or spoon mixture into warmed corn tortillas.

Favorite recipe from **USA Rice**

Nutrients per Serving: about 1 cup plus 3 tablespoons rice mixture

Calories 214	**Fiber** 3g
Fat 6g (sat 3g)	**Cholesterol** 81mg
Protein 12g	**Sodium** 356mg
Carbohydrate 27g	

Exchanges: 1-1/2 starch, 1 vegetable, 1 lean meat, 1/2 fat

Apple & Raisin Oven Pancake

low sodium

(Pictured on page 48)

- **1 large baking apple, cored and thinly sliced**
- **1/3 cup golden raisins**
- **2 tablespoons packed brown sugar**
- **1/2 teaspoon ground cinnamon**
- **4 eggs**
- **2/3 cup milk**
- **2/3 cup all-purpose flour**
- **2 tablespoons butter, melted**
- **Powdered sugar (optional)**

1. Preheat oven to 350°F. Spray 9-inch pie plate with nonstick cooking spray; set aside.

2. Combine apple, raisins, brown sugar and cinnamon in medium bowl. Transfer to prepared pie plate. Bake, uncovered, 10 to 15 minutes or until apple begins to soften. Remove from oven. *Increase oven temperature to 450°F.*

3. Meanwhile, whisk eggs, milk, flour and butter in medium bowl until blended. Pour batter over apple mixture. Bake 15 minutes or until pancake is golden brown. Invert onto serving dish. Sprinkle with powdered sugar, if desired. Cut into 6 wedges before serving.

Makes 6 servings

Nutrients per Serving: 1 wedge

Calories 202	**Fiber** 1g
Fat 8g (sat 4g)	**Cholesterol** 153mg
Protein 7g	**Sodium** 89mg
Carbohydrate 27g	

Exchanges: 1-1/2 starch, 1/2 fruit, 1/2 lean meat, 1 fat

Tip

A firmer variety of apples, such as the Granny Smith used to make this oven pancake, is better for baking than softer varieties like the McIntosh. Firmer varieties can withstand the heat of baking and cooking.

Breakfast Banana Split

low fat low sodium cooking for 1 or 2

Quick Recipe   *(Pictured below)*

- **1 small banana *or* 1/2 medium banana**
- **3 strawberries, sliced**
- **2 tablespoons fresh blueberries**
- **1 container (6 ounces) strawberry sugar-free fat-free yogurt, stirred**
- **1 tablespoon reduced-fat granola**
- **1 maraschino cherry**

Peel banana; slice lengthwise in half. Separate halves and place in serving dish. Place half of strawberries and blueberries on banana slices. Gently spoon yogurt over berries. Top with remaining berries; sprinkle with granola. Garnish with cherry.   *Makes 1 serving*

Nutrients per Serving: 1 banana split

Calories 210	**Fiber** 4g
Fat 1g (sat <1g)	**Cholesterol** 5mg
Protein 9g	**Sodium** 130mg
Carbohydrate 45g	

Exchanges: 1/2 starch, 1-1/2 fruit, 1 milk

Breakfast Banana Split

Ham & Cheddar Frittata

Quick Recipe   *(Pictured on page 48)*

   3/4 cup egg substitute
    3 egg whites
   1/2 teaspoon salt
   1/2 teaspoon black pepper
 1-1/2 cups (4 ounces) frozen broccoli florets, thawed
    6 ounces lean smoked ham, cut into 1/2-inch cubes (about 1-1/4 cups)
   1/3 cup drained bottled roasted red bell pepper strips
    1 teaspoon butter
   1/2 cup shredded reduced-fat sharp Cheddar cheese

1. Preheat broiler.

2. Beat egg substitute, egg whites, salt and black pepper in large bowl until blended. Stir in broccoli, ham and roasted red bell pepper strips.

3. Melt butter over medium heat in 10-inch ovenproof skillet with sloping side. Pour egg mixture into skillet; cover. Cook 5 to 6 minutes or until eggs are set around edge. (Center will be wet.)

4. Uncover; sprinkle cheese over frittata. Transfer skillet to broiler; broil 5 inches from heat 2 minutes or until eggs are set in center and cheese is melted. Let stand 5 minutes. Cut into 4 wedges to serve.   *Makes 4 servings*

Nutrients per Serving: 1 frittata wedge

Calories 167	**Fiber** 1g
Fat 8g (sat 3g)	**Cholesterol** 24mg
Protein 20g	**Sodium** 980mg
Carbohydrate 3g	

Exchanges: 1/2 vegetable, 3 lean meat

Eggs Benedict

Quick Recipe   *(Pictured on page 48)*

    Mock Hollandaise Sauce (recipe follows)
    4 eggs
    2 English muffins, halved
  12 to 16 fresh spinach leaves, washed and stemmed
    4 slices lean cooked Canadian bacon (about 1 ounce each), heated
    4 fresh tomato slices, cut 1/4 inch thick
    Paprika

1. Prepare Mock Hollandaise Sauce. Set aside.

2. Bring 6 cups water to a boil in large saucepan over high heat. Reduce heat to a simmer. Carefully break 1 egg into small dish and slide egg into water. Repeat with remaining 3 eggs. Simmer, uncovered, about 5 minutes or until yolks are just set.

3. Meanwhile, toast muffin halves; place on serving plates. Top each muffin half with 3 to 4 spinach leaves, 1 Canadian bacon slice, 1 tomato slice and 1 egg. Spoon 3 tablespoons Mock Hollandaise Sauce over egg; sprinkle with paprika.   *Makes 4 servings*

Mock Hollandaise Sauce

    4 ounces fat-free cream cheese
    3 tablespoons plain fat-free yogurt
    1 tablespoon lemon juice
    1 teaspoon Dijon mustard

Process all ingredients in food processor or blender until smooth. Heat in small saucepan over medium-high heat until hot.
   Makes about 3/4 cup sauce

Nutrients per Serving: 1 open-faced sandwich (with 3 tablespoons sauce)

Calories 230	**Fiber** 2g
Fat 8g (sat 3g)	**Cholesterol** 228mg
Protein 20g	**Sodium** 817mg
Carbohydrate 19g	

Exchanges: 1 starch, 1/2 vegetable, 2 lean meat, 1/2 fat

Breakfast Tacos

Quick Recipe   *(Pictured below)*

Nonstick cooking spray

1/2 cup egg substitute

1/2 teaspoon taco seasoning mix

2 regular-sized taco shells *or* 6 mini taco shells

2 tablespoons shredded reduced-fat Cheddar cheese

2 tablespoons salsa

2 tablespoons chopped fresh parsley

Sliced green onion and shredded lettuce (optional)

1. Coat small skillet with cooking spray. Heat over medium-low heat. Pour egg substitute into skillet; cook, stirring often, until desired doneness is reached. Season with taco seasoning.

2. Heat taco shells according to package directions; cool slightly. Spoon egg mixture into taco shells. Top each taco with cheese, salsa, parsley and green onion and lettuce, if desired.   *Makes 2 servings*

Nutrients per Serving: 1 regular-sized taco or 3 mini tacos

Calories 141	**Fiber** 1g
Fat 6g (sat 1g)	**Cholesterol** 2mg
Protein 11g	**Sodium** 411mg
Carbohydrate 11g	

Exchanges: 1 starch, 1 lean meat

Breakfast Tacos

Spicy Sausage Skillet Breakfast

Quick Recipe   (Pictured at right)

> **2 bags SUCCESS® Rice**
>   **Vegetable cooking spray**
> **1 pound bulk turkey sausage**
> **1/2 cup chopped onion**
> **1 can (10 ounces) tomatoes with green chilies, undrained**
> **1 tablespoon chili powder**
> **1 cup (4 ounces) shredded reduced-fat Monterey Jack cheese**

Prepare rice according to package directions.

Lightly spray large skillet with cooking spray. Crumble sausage into prepared skillet. Cook over medium heat until lightly browned, stirring occasionally. Add onion; cook until tender. Stir in tomatoes, chili powder and rice; simmer 2 minutes. Reduce heat to low. Simmer until no liquid remains, about 8 minutes, stirring occasionally. Sprinkle with cheese.

Makes 6 to 8 servings

Nutrients per Serving: 3/4 cup (based on 6 servings)

Calories 314	**Fiber** 1g
Fat 13g (sat 5g)	**Cholesterol** 72mg
Protein 21g	**Sodium** 825mg
Carbohydrate 32g	

Exchanges: 2 starch, 2 lean meat, 1-1/2 fat

Tip

The widely available unaged version of Monterey Jack cheese is buttery-ivory in color, semisoft in texture and has a mild, somewhat bland flavor reminiscent of American Muenster. It has high moisture and good melting properties, making it excellent for sandwiches as well as cooked dishes.

Breakfast in a Cup

meatless

Quick Recipe

> **3 cups cooked rice**
> **1 cup (4 ounces) shredded Cheddar cheese, divided**
> **1 can (4 ounces) diced green chilies**
> **1 jar (2 ounces) diced pimientos, drained**
> **1/3 cup skim milk**
> **2 eggs, beaten**
> **1/2 teaspoon ground cumin**
> **1/2 teaspoon salt**
> **1/2 teaspoon ground black pepper**
>   **Vegetable cooking spray**

Combine rice, 1/2 cup cheese, chilies, pimientos, milk, eggs, cumin, salt and pepper in large bowl. Evenly divide mixture into 12 muffin cups coated with cooking spray. Sprinkle with remaining 1/2 cup cheese. Bake at 400°F. for 15 minutes or until set.   *Makes 12 servings*

Hint: Breakfast cups may be stored in the freezer in a freezer bag or tightly sealed container. To reheat frozen breakfast cups, microwave each cup on HIGH 1 minute.

Favorite recipe from **USA Rice**

Nutrients per Serving: 1 muffin-sized cup

Calories 107	**Fiber** <1g
Fat 4g (sat 2g)	**Cholesterol** 45mg
Protein 5g	**Sodium** 206mg
Carbohydrate 12g	

Exchanges: 1 starch, 1/2 lean meat, 1/2 fat

Breakfast Burger

Breakfast Burger

Quick Recipe   *(Pictured above)*

    3/4 pound 93% lean ground turkey
    1/2 cup minced red bell pepper
    1/2 cup minced green bell pepper
      2 teaspoons dried onion flakes
    1/2 teaspoon black pepper
      1 teaspoon dried parsley flakes
        Nonstick cooking spray
      4 whole wheat English muffins
      8 large spinach leaves, washed and
        stemmed
      4 slices (1 ounce each) reduced-fat
        Cheddar cheese

1. Mix ground turkey, bell peppers, dried onion flakes, black pepper and parsley in large bowl. Form 4 patties and spray with cooking spray.

2. Cook patties in nonstick skillet over medium heat 7 minutes or until lightly browned on bottom. Turn patties; cook 7 minutes. Add 2 tablespoons water; cover and cook 3 minutes.

3. Toast English muffins lightly. Layer 2 spinach leaves, turkey burger and 1 cheese slice on English muffin half; top with other half of English muffin. Repeat with remaining burgers and ingredients to make 4 sandwiches.

Makes 4 servings

Nutrients per Serving: 1 sandwich

Calories 300
Fat 6g (sat 2g)
Protein 31g
Carbohydrate 30g

Fiber 5g
Cholesterol 30mg
Sodium 576mg

Exchanges: 2 starch, 3 lean meat

ɔə ɔə ɔə

Country Breakfast Cereal

low fat   low sodium

Quick Recipe

      3 cups cooked brown rice
      2 cups skim milk
    1/2 cup raisins or chopped prunes
      1 tablespoon margarine (optional)
      1 teaspoon ground cinnamon
    1/8 teaspoon salt
        Honey or brown sugar (optional)
        Fresh fruit (optional)

Combine rice, milk, raisins, margarine, cinnamon and salt in 2- to 3-quart saucepan. Bring to a boil; stir once or twice. Reduce heat to medium-low; cover and simmer 8 to 10 minutes or until thickened. Serve with honey and fresh fruit.   *Makes 6 servings*

Favorite recipe from **USA Rice**

Nutrients per Serving: about 1 cup cereal (without margarine, honey or fresh fruit)

Calories 179
Fat 1g (sat <1g)
Protein 6g
Carbohydrate 38g

Fiber 3g
Cholesterol 2mg
Sodium 98mg

Exchanges: 1-1/2 starch, 1/2 milk, 1/2 fruit

Light Sausage & Sassy Scrambled Eggs

low carb

Quick Recipe

- 1 package **JENNIE-O TURKEY STORE®
  Breakfast Sausage Links**
- **Butter-flavor cooking spray**
- **1-3/4 cups liquid egg substitute** *or* **8 large egg
  whites plus 2 large eggs**
- **1/4 cup skim milk**
- **1/2 cup finely diced red bell pepper**
- **1/2 cup thinly sliced green onions**
- **3/4 teaspoon salt (optional)**
- **3/4 teaspoon hot pepper sauce**
- **1/2 cup (2 ounces) shredded low-fat
  Cheddar cheese**

Cook sausages according to package directions. Meanwhile, coat large deep nonstick skillet with cooking spray; heat over medium-high heat. In medium bowl, beat together egg substitute, milk, bell pepper, green onions, salt, if desired, and pepper sauce. Pour into skillet. Cook, stirring occasionally, until eggs are set, 5 to 6 minutes; sprinkle with cheese and serve with sausages.   *Makes 7 servings*

Nutrients per Serving: 2 sausages with about 1/3 cup egg mixture topped with about 1 tablespoon cheese

Calories 217	**Fiber** <1g
Fat 13g (sat 4g)	**Cholesterol** 51mg
Protein 20g	**Sodium** 601mg
Carbohydrate 4g	

Exchanges: 1 vegetable, 3 lean meat, 1/2 fat

Tip

For a tasty change of pace, try substituting part-skim mozzarella cheese for the Cheddar in this scrumptious skillet dish. Season the eggs with a dash of basil or oregano.

Cinnamon Fruit Crunch

low sodium **high fiber**

Quick Recipe   *(Pictured below)*

- **1 cup low-fat granola cereal**
- **1/4 cup sliced almonds, toasted***
- **1 tablespoon butter**
- **2 tablespoons plus 1 teaspoon packed
  brown sugar, divided**
- **2-1/4 teaspoons ground cinnamon, divided**
- **1/2 cup vanilla fat-free yogurt**
- **1/8 teaspoon ground nutmeg**
- **2 cans (16 ounces each) mixed fruit
  chunks in juice, drained**

*To toast almonds, spread in single layer on baking sheet. Bake in preheated 350°F oven 8 to 10 minutes or until golden brown, stirring frequently.

1. Combine granola and almonds in small bowl. Melt butter in small saucepan. Blend in 2 tablespoons brown sugar and 2 teaspoons cinnamon. Toss with granola and almonds; cool.

2. Combine yogurt, 1 teaspoon brown sugar, 1/4 teaspoon cinnamon and nutmeg in small bowl. Top individual servings of fruit with yogurt mixture. Sprinkle granola mixture over top.

                Makes 6 servings

Nutrients per Serving: about 1/2 cup mixed fruit with 1 tablespoon yogurt mixture and 2 tablespoons granola mixture

Calories 259	**Fiber** 6g
Fat 6g (sat 1g)	**Cholesterol** 1mg
Protein 4g	**Sodium** 109mg
Carbohydrate 48g	

Exchanges: 2 starch, 1 fruit, 1 fat

Cinnamon Fruit Crunch

Breakfast Pizza

(Pictured at right)

1 package (10 ounces) refrigerated
   biscuits
1/2 pound turkey bacon slices
2 tablespoons butter
2 tablespoons all-purpose flour
1/4 teaspoon salt
1/8 teaspoon black pepper
1-1/2 cups 2% milk
1/2 cup shredded reduced-fat sharp
   Cheddar cheese
1/4 cup sliced green onions
1/4 cup chopped red bell pepper

1. Preheat oven to 350°F. Spray 13×9-inch baking dish with nonstick cooking spray.

2. Separate biscuit dough; arrange in rectangle on lightly floured surface. Roll into 14×10-inch rectangle. Place in prepared dish; pat edges up sides of dish. Bake 15 minutes. Remove from oven.

3. Meanwhile, place bacon in single layer in large skillet; cook over medium heat until crisp. Remove from skillet; drain on paper towels. Crumble; set aside.

4. Melt butter in medium saucepan over medium heat. Stir in flour, salt and black pepper until smooth. Gradually stir in milk; cook and stir until thickened. Stir in cheese until melted. Spread sauce evenly over baked crust. Arrange bacon, green onions and bell pepper over sauce.

5. Bake, uncovered, 20 minutes or until crust is golden brown. Cut into 6 wedges before serving.   *Makes 6 servings*

Nutrients per Serving: 1 pizza wedge

Calories 280	**Fiber** 1g
Fat 14g (sat 6g)	**Cholesterol** 54mg
Protein 10g	**Sodium** 793mg
Carbohydrate 29g	

Exchanges: 2 starch, 1/2 lean meat, 2-1/2 fat

Orange Breakfast Loaf

low
fat

1 cup water
1/3 cup orange juice
2 tablespoons canola oil
1 teaspoon salt
2 cups all-purpose flour
1 cup uncooked old-fashioned oats
1 cup whole wheat flour
1/2 cup dried cranberries
2 tablespoons sugar
1 teaspoon freshly grated orange peel
2 teaspoons active dry yeast

Bread Machine Directions

1. Measuring carefully, place all ingredients in bread machine pan in order specified by owner's manual.

2. Program basic or white cycle and desired crust setting; press start. Remove baked bread from pan; cool on wire rack.
          Makes 12 servings (1 [1-1/2-pound] loaf)

Nutrients per Serving: 1 slice

Calories 184	**Fiber** 3g
Fat 3g (sat <1g)	**Cholesterol** 0mg
Protein 5g	**Sodium** 195mg
Carbohydrate 35g	

Exchanges: 2 starch, 1/2 fruit, 1/2 fat

Tip

One medium orange yields 1/3 to 1/2 cup juice, while its rind yields 1 to 2 tablespoons grated peel. Before grating, scrub the orange with soap and water to remove its waxy coating and any lingering residues. Be sure to grate only the outer orange layer and avoid the bitter white pith underneath! Any leftover grated peel may be tightly wrapped and frozen for later use.

Breakfast Pizza

Main Dishes

ම ම ම

Broiled Caribbean Sea Bass

(Pictured at left)

6 skinless sea bass or striped bass fillets (5 to 6 ounces each), about 1/2 inch thick
1/3 cup chopped fresh cilantro
2 tablespoons olive oil
2 tablespoons fresh lime juice
2 teaspoons hot pepper sauce
2 cloves garlic, minced
1 package (7 ounces) black bean and rice mix
Lime slices

1. Place fish in shallow dish. Combine cilantro, oil, lime juice, pepper sauce and garlic in small bowl; pour over fish. Cover; marinate in refrigerator 30 minutes, but no longer than 2 hours.

2. Prepare black bean and rice mix according to package directions; keep warm.

3. Preheat broiler. Discard marinade. Place fish on rack of broiler pan. Broil 4 to 5 inches from heat 8 to 10 minutes or until fish is opaque. Serve fish with black beans and rice and lime slices.

Makes 6 servings

Nutrients per Serving: 1 sea bass fillet with 1/2 cup black beans and rice

Calories 291	**Fiber** 2g
Fat 7g (sat 1g)	**Cholesterol** 58mg
Protein 31g	**Sodium** 684mg
Carbohydrate 25g	

Exchanges: 1-1/2 starch, 4 lean meat

Clockwise from top left: *Baked Bean Stew (page 68), Fiesta Beef Enchiladas (page 75), Chicken Nuggets with Barbecue Dipping Sauce (page 72) and Broiled Caribbean Sea Bass*

Cilantro-Lime Chicken

low carb

Quick Recipe   *(Pictured at right)*

4 boneless skinless chicken breasts (about 1/4 pound each)

2 small onions

1 large lime

2 tablespoons canola oil

1 or 2 small green or red jalapeño peppers,* seeded and sliced

1 small piece fresh gingerroot (1 inch long), peeled and thinly sliced

2 tablespoons chopped fresh cilantro

2 tablespoons reduced-sodium soy sauce

1 to 2 teaspoons sugar

   Warmed tortillas or hot cooked rice (optional)

   Fresh cilantro sprigs, grated lime peel and red jalapeño pepper* strips (optional)

*Jalapeño peppers can sting and irritate the skin, so wear rubber gloves when handling peppers and do not touch your eyes.

1. Cut each chicken breast into 8 pieces. Cut each onion into 8 wedges.

2. Remove 3 strips of peel from lime with vegetable peeler. Cut lime peel into very fine shreds. Juice lime; measure 2 tablespoons juice. Set aside.

3. Heat wok or large skillet over medium-high heat 1 minute or until hot. Drizzle oil into wok and heat 30 seconds. Add chicken, jalapeño and gingerroot; stir-fry about 3 minutes or until chicken is no longer pink. Reduce heat to medium. Add onions; stir-fry 5 minutes.

4. Add reserved lime peel, 2 tablespoons lime juice and chopped cilantro; stir-fry 1 minute. Add soy sauce and sugar to taste; stir-fry until well mixed and heated through. Transfer to serving dish. Serve with warmed tortillas, if desired, and garnish with cilantro, lime peel and red jalapeño pepper.   *Makes 4 servings*

Nutrients per Serving: 1 cup chicken mixture

Calories 216	**Fiber** 1g
Fat 8g (sat 1g)	**Cholesterol** 66mg
Protein 28g	**Sodium** 313mg
Carbohydrate 7g	

Exchanges: 1 vegetable, 3-1/2 lean meat

Grilled Pork Tenderloin with Tomato-Mango Salsa

2 boneless pork tenderloins (about 3/4 pound each), trimmed of fat

1/3 cup reduced-sodium teriyaki sauce

2 medium tomatoes, seeded and diced

1 cup diced peeled mango

1/2 cup minced yellow or green bell pepper

1/4 cup hot jalapeño jelly, melted

2 tablespoons white wine vinegar

1. Spray cold grid of grill with nonstick cooking spray. Prepare grill for direct grilling.

2. Rub pork tenderloins all over with teriyaki sauce; let stand 5 minutes.

3. Combine tomatoes, mango, bell pepper, jelly and vinegar in medium bowl; mix well. Set aside.

4. Grill pork, covered, over medium-hot coals 20 to 25 minutes or until meat thermometer inserted into thickest part of meat registers 160°F, turning once. Slice and serve with salsa.
          Makes 6 servings

Nutrients per Serving: about 2-1/2 ounces pork (cooked weight) with about 1/4 cup plus 2 tablespoons salsa

Calories 222	**Fiber** 1g
Fat 4g (sat 1g)	**Cholesterol** 66mg
Protein 25g	**Sodium** 444mg
Carbohydrate 21g	

Exchanges: 1 starch, 1/2 fruit, 1/2 vegetable, 3 lean meat

Cilantro-Lime Chicken

Buttery Pepper and Citrus Broiled Fish

Buttery Pepper and Citrus Broiled Fish

low fat | low carb

Quick Recipe   *(Pictured above)*

**3 tablespoons MOLLY MCBUTTER®
   Flavored Sprinkles**
**1 tablespoon MRS. DASH® Lemon Pepper
   Blend**
1 tablespoon lime juice
2 teaspoons honey
1 pound boneless white fish fillets

Combine first 4 ingredients in small bowl; mix well. Broil fish 6 to 8 inches from heat, turning once. Spread with Lemon Pepper mixture. Broil an additional 4 to 5 minutes.

Makes 4 servings

Nutrients per Serving: 1 fillet

Calories 106	**Fiber** <1g
Fat 1g (sat <1g)	**Cholesterol** 23mg
Protein 17g	**Sodium** 462mg
Carbohydrate 7g	

Exchanges: 1/2 starch, 2-1/2 lean meat

Baked Bean Stew

high fiber

Quick Recipe   *(Pictured on page 64)*

1 cup chopped onion
1 cup chopped green bell pepper
1 tablespoon vegetable oil
**12 ounces boneless skinless chicken
   breasts or tenders, cut into 1/2-inch
   pieces**
**2 cans (15 ounces each) baked beans or
   pork and beans**
**1 can (15 ounces) garbanzo beans or
   black-eyes or 1-1/2 cups cooked
   dry-packaged garbanzo beans or
   black-eyes, rinsed, drained**
**1 can (14-1/2 ounces) diced tomatoes
   with roasted garlic, undrained**
3/4 teaspoon dried sage leaves
1/2 teaspoon ground cumin
   Salt and pepper, to taste

1. Cook onion and green bell pepper in oil in large saucepan until tender, 3 to 4 minutes. Add chicken and cook over medium heat until browned, 3 to 4 minutes.

2. Add beans, tomatoes and herbs to saucepan; heat to boiling. Reduce heat and simmer, uncovered, 8 to 10 minutes. Season to taste with salt and pepper.   *Makes 8 servings*

Note: Frozen chopped onion and green bell pepper can be used. Stew can be prepared 1 to 2 days in advance; refrigerate, covered. Stew can also be frozen up to 2 months.

Favorite recipe from **American Dry Bean Board**

Nutrients per Serving: 1-1/2 cups stew (without salt and pepper seasoning)

Calories 270	**Fiber** 9g
Fat 5g (sat 1g)	**Cholesterol** 32mg
Protein 19g	**Sodium** 864mg
Carbohydrate 40g	

Exchanges: 2 starch, 1-1/2 vegetable, 1-1/2 lean meat, 1/2 fat

Fajitas

Fajita Marinade (recipe follows)
1 beef flank steak (about 1 pound)
Salsa Cruda (recipe follows)
6 large (10-inch) flour tortillas *or* 12
    (7-inch) flour tortillas
4 medium bell peppers, any color, halved
1 large bunch green onions
1 cup coarsely chopped fresh cilantro
1 medium avocado, thinly sliced
    (optional)
6 tablespoons reduced-fat sour cream
    (optional)

1. Combine Fajita Marinade and flank steak in resealable plastic bag. Press air from bag and seal. Refrigerate 30 minutes or up to 24 hours.

2. Prepare Salsa Cruda; set aside. Wrap tortillas in foil in stacks of 3; set aside.

3. Drain marinade from meat into small saucepan. Bring to a boil over high heat; cook and stir 5 minutes. Remove from heat.

4. Spray cold grid of grill with nonstick cooking spray. Adjust grid 4 to 6 inches above heat. Preheat grill to medium heat. Place steak in center of grid. Grill, uncovered, 17 to 21 minutes for medium-rare to medium or until desired doneness is reached. Baste steak frequently with marinade; turn once.

5. Place bell peppers, skin side down, around meat. Grill bell peppers 6 minutes or until skin is spotted brown. Turn over and continue grilling 6 to 8 minutes or until tender. Move to sides of grill to keep warm while steak finishes grilling.

6. During the last 4 minutes of grilling, brush green onions with remaining marinade and place on grid; grill 1 to 2 minutes or until browned in spots. Turn over; grill 1 to 2 minutes or until tender.

7. Place packets of tortillas on grid; heat about 5 minutes. Slice bell peppers and onions into thin, 2-inch-long pieces. Thinly slice steak across the grain.

8. Place each tortilla on plate. Place meat, bell peppers, onions, Salsa Cruda and cilantro in center of each tortilla. Fold bottom 3 inches of each tortilla up over filling; roll up to enclose. Serve with avocado and sour cream, if desired.

Makes 6 servings

Fajita Marinade

1/2 cup lime juice
1 tablespoon minced garlic
1 tablespoon dried oregano
2 teaspoons ground cumin
2 teaspoons black pepper

Combine lime juice, garlic, oregano, cumin and black pepper in 1-cup glass measure.

Makes 2/3 cup

Salsa Cruda

1 cup chopped seeded fresh tomato
2 tablespoons minced onion
2 tablespoons minced fresh cilantro
2 tablespoons lime juice
1/2 jalapeño pepper,* seeded and minced
3 cloves garlic, minced

Jalapeño peppers can sting and irritate the skin, so wear rubber gloves when handling peppers and do not touch your eyes.

Combine all ingredients in small bowl.

Makes 6 servings

Nutrients per Serving: 1 fajita with 3 tablespoons plus 1 teaspoon Salsa Cruda

Calories 304	Fiber 3g
Fat 9g (sat 4g)	Cholesterol 44mg
Protein 30g	Sodium 198mg
Carbohydrate 25g	

Exchanges: 1 starch, 2 vegetable, 3 lean meat, 1/2 fat

Meatballs with Sweet and Sassy Sauce

(Pictured at right)

1 pound ground turkey breast
1 pound ground sirloin
2 eggs, slightly beaten
3/4 cup saltine cracker crumbs
1/4 cup grated Asiago cheese
3 tablespoons minced onion
2 cloves garlic, minced
1/4 teaspoon ground black pepper

• Preheat oven to 425°F. Combine all ingredients. Shape into 1-1/2-inch-diameter meatballs. Place on 15×10-inch baking pan. Bake 18 to 20 minutes. Remove pan from oven to wire rack. *Makes 8 servings*

Sweet and Sassy Sauce

1 cup medium salsa
1 can (14-3/4 ounces) reduced-fat and reduced-sodium chicken broth
1 can (12 ounces) tomato paste
1/4 cup EQUAL® SPOONFUL*
2 tablespoons lemon juice
2 teaspoons Jamaican jerk seasoning
Hot cooked pasta or rice (optional)

May substitute 6 packets EQUAL® sweetener.

• Combine all ingredients in large saucepan with cover. Place cooked meatballs in sauce. Heat to simmer over medium heat. Simmer, covered, 20 minutes to blend flavors. Serve over hot cooked pasta or rice, if desired.

Nutrients per Serving: 6 meatballs with 1/2 cup sauce (without noodles)

Calories 266	**Fiber** 3g
Fat 10g (sat 3g)	**Cholesterol** 131mg
Protein 28g	**Sodium** 461mg
Carbohydrate 16g	

Exchanges: 1 starch, 3-1/2 lean meat

Light Buenos Burritos

high fiber

Quick Recipe

Cooking spray
1/2 cup chopped onion
2 teaspoons bottled or fresh minced garlic
1 package JENNIE-O TURKEY STORE® Breast Strips
1 tablespoon Mexican seasoning or 2 teaspoons chili powder plus 1 teaspoon ground cumin
1/2 cup salsa
1 can (16 ounces) black beans, rinsed and drained
1 cup (4 ounces) shredded low-fat Cheddar cheese
1/2 cup chopped fresh cilantro or sliced green onions
6 (10-inch) fat-free flour tortillas, warmed

Coat large non-stick skillet with cooking spray; heat over medium heat. Add onion and garlic; cook 5 minutes, stirring occasionally. Toss turkey with seasoning; add to skillet. Stir-fry 2 minutes. Add salsa and beans; simmer about 6 minutes or until turkey is no longer pink in center, stirring occasionally. Remove from heat; stir in cheese and cilantro. Spoon down center of warm tortillas. Fold bottom of tortilla over filling, fold in sides and roll up.

Makes 6 servings

Nutrients per Serving: 1 burrito

Calories 342	**Fiber** 13g
Fat 6g (sat 3g)	**Cholesterol** 48mg
Protein 32g	**Sodium** 929mg
Carbohydrate 39g	

Exchanges: 2-1/2 starch, 1/2 vegetable, 3-1/2 lean meat

Meatballs with Sweet and Sassy Sauce

Chicken Nuggets with Barbecue Dipping Sauce

Quick Recipe   *(Pictured on page 64)*

- **1 pound boneless skinless chicken breasts**
- **1/4 cup all-purpose flour**
- **1/4 teaspoon salt**
- **Dash black pepper**
- **2 cups crushed reduced-fat baked cheese crackers**
- **1 teaspoon dried oregano**
- **1 egg white**
- **1 tablespoon water**
- **3 tablespoons barbecue sauce**
- **2 tablespoons no-sugar-added peach or apricot fruit spread**

1. Preheat oven to 400°F. Cut chicken into 32 pieces.

2. Place flour, salt and pepper in large resealable plastic bag. Combine cracker crumbs and oregano in shallow bowl. Whisk together egg white and water in small bowl.

3. Place 6 to 8 chicken pieces in bag with flour mixture; seal bag. Shake until chicken is well coated. Remove chicken from bag; shake off excess flour. Coat all sides of chicken pieces with egg white mixture. Roll in crumb mixture. Place in shallow baking pan. Repeat with remaining chicken pieces. Bake 10 to 13 minutes or until golden brown.

4. Meanwhile, combine barbecue sauce and fruit spread in small saucepan. Cook and stir over low heat until heated through. Serve chicken nuggets with dipping sauce.   *Makes 8 servings*

Note: To freeze chicken nuggets, cool 5 minutes on baking sheet. Wrap chicken in plastic wrap, making packages of 4 nuggets each. Place packages in freezer container or plastic freezer bag. Freeze. To reheat nuggets, preheat oven to 325°F. Unwrap nuggets. Place nuggets on ungreased baking sheet. Bake 13 to 15 minutes or until hot. Or, place 4 nuggets on microwave-safe plate. Microwave on DEFROST (30%) 2-1/2 to 3-1/2 minutes or until hot, turning once.

Hint: Per serving, combine 1-1/2 teaspoons barbecue sauce and 1/2 teaspoon fruit spread in small microwave-safe dish. Microwave on HIGH 10 to 15 seconds or until hot.

Nutrients per Serving: 4 nuggets with about 2 teaspoons sauce

Calories 167	**Fiber** <1g
Fat 4g (sat 1g)	**Cholesterol** 61mg
Protein 14g	**Sodium** 313mg
Carbohydrate 16g	

Exchanges: 1 starch, 1-1/2 lean meat

ॐ ॐ ॐ

Pork Roast with Dijon Tarragon Glaze

low sodium   low carb

- **1/3 cup reduced-sodium chicken or vegetable broth**
- **2 tablespoons Dijon mustard**
- **2 tablespoons lemon juice**
- **1 teaspoon minced tarragon**
- **1 boneless pork loin roast (about 1-1/2 pounds), trimmed of fat**
- **1 teaspoon ground paprika**
- **1/2 teaspoon freshly ground black pepper**

1. Preheat oven to 350°F. For glaze, combine broth, mustard, lemon juice and tarragon in small bowl; set aside.

2. Line roasting pan with foil. Place pork on rack in prepared pan. Sprinkle roast with paprika and pepper. Bake 15 minutes. Remove roast from oven. Spoon glaze evenly over roast; bake 20 minutes. Baste roast with pan drippings. Bake 20 to 30 minutes or until internal temperature reaches 160°F. Remove roast from oven; let stand 15 minutes before slicing.   *Make 6 servings*

Nutrients per Serving: 3 ounces pork (cooked weight) with 2 teaspoons glaze

Calories 113	**Fiber** <1g
Fat 4g (sat 1g)	**Cholesterol** 49mg
Protein 17g	**Sodium** 126mg
Carbohydrate 1g	

Exchanges: 2 lean meat

Hazelnut-Coated Salmon Steaks

Quick Recipe   *(Pictured below)*

1/4 cup hazelnuts
4 salmon steaks (about 5 ounces each)
1 tablespoon apple butter
1 tablespoon Dijon mustard
1/4 teaspoon dried thyme
1/8 teaspoon black pepper

1. Preheat oven to 375°F. Place hazelnuts on baking sheet; bake 8 minutes or until lightly browned. Quickly transfer nuts to clean dry dish towel. Fold towel over nuts; rub vigorously to remove as much of skins as possible. Using food processor, finely chop hazelnuts.

2. *Increase oven temperature to 450°F.* Place salmon in single layer in baking dish. Combine apple butter, mustard, thyme and pepper in small bowl; brush onto salmon. Top each steak with hazelnuts.

3. Bake 14 to 16 minutes or until salmon begins to flake when tested with fork. Serve with herbed rice and steamed sugar snap peas, if desired.   *Makes 4 servings*

Nutrients per Serving: 1 salmon steak (without rice and sugar snap peas)

Calories 273	**Fiber** 1g
Fat 14g (sat 2g)	**Cholesterol** 64mg
Protein 32g	**Sodium** 161mg
Carbohydrate 4g	

Exchanges: 1/2 starch, 4-1/2 lean meat

Hazelnut-Coated Salmon Steak

Grilled Fish with Orange-Chile Salsa

Grilled Fish with Orange-Chile Salsa

 low fat | low sodium

Quick Recipe   *(Pictured above)*

3 medium oranges, peeled and sectioned* (about 1-1/4 cups segments)

1/4 cup finely diced green, red or yellow bell pepper

3 tablespoons chopped fresh cilantro, divided

3 tablespoons lime juice, divided

1 tablespoon honey

1 teaspoon minced, seeded serrano pepper *or* **1 tablespoon minced jalapeño pepper****

4 firm white fish fillets, such as orange roughy, lingcod, halibut or red snapper (about 5 ounces each)

Lime slices

Zucchini ribbons, cooked

*Canned mandarin orange segments can be substituted for fresh orange segments, if desired.

**Chile peppers can sting and irritate the skin, so wear rubber gloves when handling peppers and do not touch your eyes.

To prepare Orange-Chile Salsa, combine orange segments, bell pepper, 2 tablespoons cilantro, 2 tablespoons lime juice, honey and serrano pepper. Set aside.

Season fish fillets with remaining 1 tablespoon cilantro and 1 tablespoon lime juice. Lightly oil grid to prevent sticking. Grill fish on covered grill over medium KINGSFORD® Briquets 5 minutes. Turn and top with lime slices, if desired. Grill about 5 minutes until fish flakes easily when tested with fork. Serve with Orange-Chile Salsa. Garnish with zucchini ribbons.   *Makes 4 servings*

Note: Allow about 10 minutes grilling time per inch thickness of fish fillets.

Nutrients per Serving: 1 grilled fish fillet with about 1/4 cup plus 2 tablespoons salsa

Calories 154	**Fiber** <1g
Fat 1g (sat <1g)	**Cholesterol** 28mg
Protein 21g	**Sodium** 88mg
Carbohydrate 14g	

Exchanges: 1 fruit, 3 lean meat

Tip

Lingcod is a low-fat fish with a mildly sweet flavor and firm texture. It ranges from 3 to 20 pounds and is available whole or as steaks or fillets.

Fiesta Beef Enchiladas

(Pictured on page 64)

1 pound 95% lean ground beef
1/2 cup sliced green onions
2 teaspoons minced garlic
1-1/2 cups chopped seeded fresh tomatoes, divided
1 cup cooked white or brown rice
1 cup shredded reduced-fat Mexican cheese blend or Cheddar cheese, divided
3/4 cup frozen corn, thawed
1/2 cup salsa or picante sauce
12 (6- to 7-inch) corn tortillas
1 can (10 ounces) mild or hot enchilada sauce
1 cup shredded romaine lettuce

1. Preheat oven to 375°F. Spray 13×9-inch baking dish with nonstick cooking spray; set aside.

2. Brown ground beef in medium nonstick skillet over medium-high heat, stirring to separate meat; drain fat. Add green onions and garlic; cook and stir 2 minutes.

3. Add 1 cup tomatoes, rice, 1/2 cup cheese, corn and salsa to meat mixture; mix well. Spoon mixture down center of each tortilla; roll up. Place, seam side down, in prepared dish. Spoon enchilada sauce evenly over enchiladas.

4. Cover with foil; bake 20 minutes or until hot. Sprinkle with remaining 1/2 cup cheese; bake 5 minutes or until cheese melts. Top with lettuce and remaining 1/2 cup tomato.

Makes 6 servings

Nutrients per Serving: 2 enchiladas

Calories 341	**Fiber** 4g
Fat 11g (sat 5g)	**Cholesterol** 38mg
Protein 17g	**Sodium** 465mg
Carbohydrate 43g	

Exchanges: 2 starch, 2 vegetable, 2 lean meat, 1 fat

Light Shepherd's Pie

Quick Recipe

Cooking spray
2 teaspoons bottled or fresh minced garlic
1 package JENNIE-O TURKEY STORE® Extra Lean Ground Turkey Breast
1 teaspoon herbes de Provence *or* 1/2 teaspoon dried basil and 1/2 teaspoon dried thyme
1/2 teaspoon salt (optional)
1/2 teaspoon freshly ground black pepper
1 jar (12 ounces) fat-free turkey gravy
1/2 cup frozen corn kernels
1/2 cup frozen tiny peas
2-1/2 cups prepared frozen mashed potatoes (using skim milk)
1/2 cup (2 ounces) shredded low-fat Cheddar cheese

Coat 10-inch oven-proof skillet with cooking spray. (If skillet is not oven-proof, wrap handle in double thickness of aluminum foil.) Place over medium-high heat; add garlic. Crumble turkey into skillet; sprinkle with herbes de Provence, salt and pepper. Cook 5 minutes or until no longer pink, stirring occasionally. Add gravy, corn and peas; simmer, uncovered, 5 minutes or until vegetables are defrosted and mixture is very hot. Spoon mashed potatoes around edge of mixture, leaving 3-inch opening in center. Transfer skillet to broiler and broil about 4 to 5 inches from heat source for 2 to 3 minutes or until mixture is bubbly. Sprinkle with cheese; return to broiler and broil 1 minute or until cheese is melted.   *Makes 6 servings*

Nutrients per Serving: 1 cup pie

Calories 263	**Fiber** 2g
Fat 6g (sat 2g)	**Cholesterol** 47mg
Protein 27g	**Sodium** 563mg
Carbohydrate 18g	

Exchanges: 1 starch, 3 lean meat

Broccoli, Scallop and Linguine Toss

Quick Recipe   *(Pictured at right)*

3/4 pound fresh or frozen scallops, thawed
2 medium onions, cut in half lengthwise and sliced
1 cup apple juice
2 tablespoons dry white wine
2 cloves garlic, minced
1-1/2 to 2 teaspoons dried ground marjoram
1 teaspoon dried basil
1/4 teaspoon white pepper
3 cups fresh broccoli florets
1 tablespoon plus 1 teaspoon cornstarch
1/4 cup water
1-1/2 cups chopped seeded fresh tomatoes
1/4 cup grated Parmesan cheese
4 cups hot cooked linguine

1. Cut large scallops into 1-inch pieces. Combine onions, apple juice, wine, garlic, marjoram, basil and pepper in large skillet; bring to a boil over high heat. Add broccoli; return to a boil. Reduce heat to medium-low; cover and simmer 7 minutes. Add scallops; return to a boil. Reduce heat. Cover and simmer 1 to 2 minutes or until scallops are opaque. Remove scallops and vegetables; set aside.

2. Combine cornstarch and water in small bowl; stir into mixture in skillet. Cook and stir over medium heat until mixture boils and thickens. Cook and stir 2 minutes more. Stir in tomatoes and cheese; heat through. Return scallops and vegetables to skillet; heat through. Toss mixture with linguine.   *Makes 4 servings*

Nutrients per Serving: 2 cups

Calories 248	**Fiber** 4g
Fat 4g (sat 1g)	**Cholesterol** 33mg
Protein 22g	**Sodium** 309mg
Carbohydrate 33g	

Exchanges: 1 starch, 1/2 fruit, 1-1/2 vegetable, 2 lean meat

Red Wine & Oregano Beef Kabobs

low carb

1/4 cup finely chopped fresh parsley
1/4 cup dry red wine
2 tablespoons Worcestershire sauce
1 tablespoon reduced-sodium soy sauce
1 teaspoon dried oregano
3 cloves garlic, minced
1/2 teaspoon salt (optional)
1/2 teaspoon black pepper
3/4 pound boneless beef top sirloin steak, trimmed of fat and cut into 16 (1-inch) pieces
16 whole mushrooms (about 8 ounces total)
1 medium red onion, cut into eighths and layers separated

1. Combine parsley, wine, Worcestershire, soy sauce, oregano, garlic, salt, if desired, and pepper in small bowl; stir until well blended. Place steak, mushrooms and onion in large resealable plastic bag. Add wine mixture; toss. Seal and marinate in refrigerator 1 hour, turning frequently.

2. Soak 4 (12-inch) or 8 (6-inch) bamboo skewers in water 20 minutes to prevent burning.

3. Coat broiler rack with nonstick cooking spray. Preheat broiler. Drain marinade from bag and discard. Alternate beef, mushrooms and 2 layers of onion on skewers.

4. Arrange skewers on broiler rack. Broil 4 to 6 inches from heat source 8 to 10 minutes, turning occasionally.   *Makes 4 servings*

Nutrients per Serving: 1 (12-inch) kabob

Calories 163	**Fiber** 1g
Fat 4g (sat 1g)	**Cholesterol** 40mg
Protein 22g	**Sodium** 209mg
Carbohydrate 8g	

Exchanges: 1-1/2 vegetable, 2-1/2 lean meat

Broccoli, Scallop and Linguine Toss

Beef and Pasta Salad with Creamy Blue Cheese Dressing

Beef and Pasta Salad with Creamy Blue Cheese Dressing

high fiber

Quick Recipe　　　*(Pictured above)*

Nonstick cooking spray

3/4 pound boneless beef tenderloin or eye of round steaks, trimmed of fat

8 ounces radiatore pasta, cooked and cooled to room temperature

1-1/2 cups fresh broccoli florets, cooked crisp-tender and cooled

1 medium yellow bell pepper, cored, seeded and cut into strips

1 medium tomato, cut into wedges

1 carrot, sliced

1/2 small red onion, thinly sliced

Creamy Blue Cheese Dressing (recipe follows)

1/4 teaspoon salt

1/8 teaspoon black pepper

1. Spray small skillet with cooking spray. Heat over medium heat until hot. Add beef; cook 7 to 9 minutes or until desired doneness is reached, turning once. Cut beef into 1/4-inch slices.

2. Toss beef, pasta, broccoli, bell pepper, tomato, carrot and red onion in large bowl; drizzle with Creamy Blue Cheese Dressing and toss. Season with salt and black pepper.

Makes 4 servings

Creamy Blue Cheese Dressing

1/2 cup fat-free mayonnaise

2 tablespoons crumbled blue cheese

1 tablespoon white wine vinegar

1 teaspoon lemon juice

1/2 teaspoon dill weed

1 clove garlic, minced

Mix all ingredients in small bowl; refrigerate until ready to use. Stir before serving.

Makes about 2/3 cup

Nutrients per Serving: 2-1/2 cups salad with 2 tablespoons plus 2 teaspoons dressing

Calories 388	**Fiber** 5g
Fat 7g (sat 3g)	**Cholesterol** 52mg
Protein 29g	**Sodium** 514mg
Carbohydrate 53g	

Exchanges: 3 starch, 1-1/2 vegetable, 2-1/2 lean meat

Tip

Blue cheese has been treated with molds to form blue (or occasionally green) veins throughout, giving a strong, tangy flavor that intensifies with age. There are as many as 66 different types of blue cheese, but the most popular are Gorgonzola, Roquefort and Stilton.

Hot Shrimp with Cool Salsa

Quick Recipe   *(Pictured below right)*

- 1/4 cup salsa
- 4 tablespoons fresh lime juice, divided
- 1 teaspoon honey
- 1 clove garlic, minced
- 2 to 4 drops hot pepper sauce
- 1 pound large uncooked shrimp, peeled and deveined, with tails intact
- 1 cup finely diced honeydew melon
- 1/2 cup finely diced unpeeled cucumber
- 2 tablespoons minced fresh parsley
- 1 green onion, finely chopped
- 1-1/2 teaspoons sugar
- 1 teaspoon olive oil
- 1/4 teaspoon salt

1. To make marinade, combine salsa, 2 tablespoons lime juice, honey, garlic and hot pepper sauce in small bowl. Thread shrimp onto skewers. Brush shrimp with marinade; set aside.

2. To make salsa, combine remaining 2 tablespoons lime juice, melon, cucumber, parsley, onion, sugar, oil and salt in medium bowl; mix well.

3. Grill shrimp over medium coals 4 to 5 minutes or until shrimp turn pink, turning once. Serve with salsa.   *Makes 4 servings*

Nutrients per Serving: about 3 to 4 large shrimp with about 5 tablespoons salsa

Calories 132	**Fiber** 1g
Fat 2g (sat <1g)	**Cholesterol** 175mg
Protein 19g	**Sodium** 398mg
Carbohydrate 8g	

Exchanges: 1/2 fruit, 2-1/2 lean meat

Turkey Breast Meat Loaf

- 2 pounds 93% lean ground turkey
- 1 cup grated unpeeled zucchini
- 3/4 cup diced red bell pepper
- 3/4 cup diced green bell pepper
- 1/2 cup uncooked old-fashioned oats
- 2 eggs, beaten
- 1 tablespoon ketchup
- 1 teaspoon dried thyme
- 1 teaspoon Dijon mustard
- 1/2 teaspoon *each* salt and black pepper
- Chopped fresh parsley (optional)

1. Preheat oven to 400°F. Spray 9×5×2-inch loaf pan with nonstick cooking spray. Line bottom with waxed paper or parchment cut to fit. Spray lightly.

2. Combine all ingredients except parsley in large bowl. Form into loaf in prepared pan, pressing mixture down with spoon or spatula to pack firmly and level top.

3. Bake 1 hour or until meat thermometer inserted into center of loaf reads 165°F. Remove from oven. Let rest 15 minutes. Run spatula around edge to loosen. To unmold, place 10-inch plate on top of pan and invert. Remove waxed paper or parchment from bottom of loaf. Sprinkle with chopped parsley, if desired. Cut meat loaf into 8 (1-inch-thick) slices before serving.
    Makes 8 servings

Nutrients per Serving: 1 meat loaf slice

Calories 199	**Fiber** 1g
Fat 9g (sat 2g)	**Cholesterol** 118mg
Protein 25g	**Sodium** 284mg
Carbohydrate 6g	

Exchanges: 1/2 starch, 3 lean meat

Pork and Sweet Potato Skillet

Quick Recipe   *(Pictured at right)*

- 1 teaspoon fennel or caraway seeds
- 3/4 pound boneless pork tenderloin, trimmed of fat and cut into 1-inch cubes
- 1 tablespoon plus 1 teaspoon butter, divided
- 1/4 teaspoon salt
- 1/8 teaspoon black pepper
- 2 medium sweet potatoes, peeled and cut into 1/2-inch pieces (about 2 cups)
- 1 small onion, sliced
- 1/4 pound low-fat smoked turkey sausage, halved lengthwise and cut into 1/2-inch pieces
- 1 small red apple, cored and cut into 1/2-inch pieces
- 1/2 cup sweet-and-sour sauce
- 2 tablespoons chopped fresh parsley (optional)

1. Cook fennel seeds in large nonstick skillet over medium heat 30 seconds to 1 minute or just until seeds begin to toast.

2. Add pork and 1 teaspoon butter to skillet; cook and stir 2 to 3 minutes or until pork is no longer pink. Season with salt and pepper. Remove from skillet.

3. Add remaining 1 tablespoon butter, potatoes and onion to skillet. Cook, covered, over medium-low heat 8 to 10 minutes or until tender, stirring frequently.

4. Add pork, sausage, apple and sweet-and-sour sauce to skillet; cook and stir until heated through. Sprinkle with parsley.

Makes 4 servings

Nutrients per Serving: 1-1/2 cups

Calories 309	**Fiber** 3g
Fat 7g (sat 4g)	**Cholesterol** 71mg
Protein 22g	**Sodium** 565mg
Carbohydrate 39g	

Exchanges: 2 starch, 1/2 fruit, 1/2 vegetable, 2 lean meat

Stir-Fry Vegetable Pizza

meatless

Quick Recipe

- Nonstick cooking spray
- 1 pound (about 5 cups) fresh cut stir-fry vegetables (packaged or from the salad bar), such as broccoli, zucchini, bell peppers and red onions
- 1 (12-inch) prepared bread-style pizza crust
- 1/3 cup pizza sauce
- 1/4 teaspoon red pepper flakes (optional)
- 1-1/2 cups shredded part-skim mozzarella cheese

1. Preheat oven to 425°F.

2. Coat large nonstick skillet with cooking spray. Heat over medium-high heat 1 minute.

3. Add vegetables; stir-fry 4 to 5 minutes or until crisp-tender.

4. Place pizza crust on large baking sheet; top with pizza sauce. Sprinkle red pepper flakes over sauce, if desired. Arrange vegetables over sauce; top with cheese.

5. Bake 12 to 14 minutes or until crust is golden brown and cheese is melted. Cut into 8 wedges to serve.

Makes 4 servings

Nutrients per Serving: 2 pizza wedges

Calories 312	**Fiber** 2g
Fat 10g (sat 4g)	**Cholesterol** 29mg
Protein 21g	**Sodium** 528mg
Carbohydrate 35g	

Exchanges: 2 starch, 1 vegetable, 2 lean meat, 1 fat

Pork and Sweet Potato Skillet

Turkey & Pasta with Cilantro Pesto

Turkey & Pasta with Cilantro Pesto

Quick Recipe　　　*(Pictured above)*

1 pound turkey tenders, cut into strips
3 cloves garlic, minced
1/2 teaspoon ground cumin
1/4 teaspoon black pepper
1/4 teaspoon ground red pepper (cayenne)
2 tablespoons olive oil
2 cups chopped seeded fresh tomatoes
1/2 cup chopped fresh cilantro
1/4 cup grated Parmesan cheese
2 tablespoons orange juice
12 ounces dry linguine, cooked and kept warm

1. Combine turkey, garlic, cumin, black pepper and red pepper in medium bowl; toss to coat. Heat oil in large skillet over medium-high heat. Add turkey mixture; cook 4 to 6 minutes or until turkey is no longer pink.

2. Add tomatoes; cook 2 minutes. Stir in cilantro, cheese and orange juice; cook 1 minute.

3. Toss turkey mixture and linguine in large bowl. Serve immediately.　　*Makes 6 servings*

Nutrients per Serving: 1-1/2 cups

Calories 365	**Fiber** 1g
Fat 9g (sat 2g)	**Cholesterol** 33mg
Protein 23g	**Sodium** 112mg
Carbohydrate 48g	

Exchanges: 3 starch, 1 vegetable, 1-1/2 lean meat, 1 fat

Almost Sloppy Joes

Quick Recipe

- 1 tablespoon olive oil
- 2 medium green bell peppers, cored, seeded and chopped
- 1 medium onion, peeled and chopped
- 1 tablespoon minced peeled shallot
- 3 cloves garlic, minced
- 1 teaspoon dried Italian seasoning
- 1/2 teaspoon salt substitute
- 1/2 teaspoon ground black pepper
- 1 pound 95% lean ground beef
- 8 ounces sliced fresh mushrooms
- 1 can (15 ounces) Mexican corn, drained
- 1 can (about 14 ounces) reduced-sodium diced tomatoes
- 1 tablespoon minced fresh parsley

1. Heat oil in large nonstick skillet over medium heat. Cook bell peppers, onion, shallot and garlic with Italian seasoning, salt substitute and black pepper until tender.

2. Add beef to skillet; cook until no longer pink, stirring to break up meat. Spoon off excess fat. Add mushrooms. Cook, stirring, 2 minutes. Add corn and tomatoes; cover. Reduce heat and simmer 2 to 4 minutes. Add parsley.

Makes 8 servings

Nutrients per Serving: 1 cup sloppy joe mixture

Calories 167	**Fiber** 4g
Fat 5g (sat 2g)	**Cholesterol** 35mg
Protein 15g	**Sodium** 354mg
Carbohydrate 17g	

Exchanges: 1/2 starch, 1-1/2 vegetable, 1-1/2 lean meat

Tip

Shallots are mild-flavored members of the onion family, but they are also similar to garlic with their small, clustered bulbs and thin, papery skin. They are available year-round in most supermarkets. Choose dry shallots that are plump, firm, and show no signs of wrinkling or sprouting.

Zesty Skillet Pork Chops

- 1 teaspoon chili powder
- 1/2 teaspoon salt, divided
- 4 lean boneless pork chops (about 1-1/4 pounds), trimmed of fat
- 2 cups diced tomatoes
- 1 cup chopped green, red or yellow bell pepper
- 3/4 cup thinly sliced celery
- 1/2 cup chopped onion
- 1 tablespoon hot pepper sauce
- 1 teaspoon dried thyme
  Nonstick cooking spray
- 2 tablespoons finely chopped fresh parsley

1. Rub chili powder and 1/4 teaspoon salt evenly over 1 side of pork chops.

2. Combine tomatoes, bell pepper, celery, onion, pepper sauce and thyme in medium bowl; stir to blend.

3. Lightly coat 12-inch nonstick skillet with cooking spray. Heat over medium-high heat until hot. Add pork chops, seasoned side down; cook 1 minute.

4. Turn pork; top with tomato mixture. Bring to a boil. Reduce heat and simmer, covered, 25 minutes or until pork is tender and mixture has thickened. Transfer pork to serving plates.

5. Increase heat; bring tomato mixture to a boil and cook 2 minutes or until most of liquid has evaporated. Remove from heat; stir in parsley and remaining 1/4 teaspoon salt. Spoon tomato mixture over pork.

Makes 4 servings

Nutrients per Serving: 1 pork chop with 2/3 cup tomato mixture

Calories 172	**Fiber** 3g
Fat 7g (sat 2g)	**Cholesterol** 49mg
Protein 20g	**Sodium** 387mg
Carbohydrate 9g	

Exchanges: 2 vegetable, 2-1/2 lean meat

Spinach Stuffed Manicotti

(Pictured at right)

- **1 package (10 ounces) frozen spinach**
- **8 uncooked manicotti shells**
- **1-1/2 teaspoons olive oil**
- **1 teaspoon dried rosemary**
- **1 teaspoon dried sage**
- **1 teaspoon dried oregano**
- **1 teaspoon dried thyme**
- **1 teaspoon chopped garlic**
- **1-1/2 cups chopped seeded fresh tomatoes**
- **1/2 cup ricotta cheese**
- **1/2 cup fresh whole wheat bread crumbs**
- **2 egg whites, lightly beaten**
- **Yellow bell pepper rings and fresh sage sprig (optional)**

1. Cook spinach according to package directions. Place in colander to drain. Let stand until cool enough to handle. Squeeze spinach to remove excess moisture. Set aside.

2. Cook pasta according to package directions, omitting salt; drain. Rinse under cold running water until cool enough to handle; drain.

3. Preheat oven to 350°F.

4. Heat oil in medium saucepan over medium heat. Cook and stir rosemary, sage, oregano, thyme and garlic in hot oil about 1 minute. (Do not let herbs turn brown.) Add tomatoes; reduce heat to low. Simmer, uncovered, 10 minutes, stirring occasionally.

5. Combine spinach, cheese and crumbs in medium bowl. Fold in egg whites. Fill cooked shells with spinach mixture.

6. Place one third of tomato mixture in 13×9-inch baking dish. Arrange manicotti in dish. Pour remaining tomato mixture over top. Cover with foil. Bake 30 minutes or until bubbly. Garnish with yellow bell pepper rings and sage sprig. *Makes 4 servings*

Nutrients per Serving: 2 stuffed manicotti

Calories 246	**Fiber** 5g
Fat 6g (sat 3g)	**Cholesterol** 13mg
Protein 14g	**Sodium** 160mg
Carbohydrate 36g	

Exchanges: 2 starch, 1-1/2 vegetable, 1 lean meat, 1/2 fat

ঌ ঌ ঌ

Halibut with Cilantro and Lime

Quick Recipe

- **1 pound halibut, tuna or swordfish fillets**
- **2 tablespoons fresh lime juice**
- **1 teaspoon cornstarch**
- **2 tablespoons reduced-sodium soy sauce**
- **1/2 teaspoon minced fresh gingerroot**
- **1/2 teaspoon canola oil**
- **1/2 cup slivered red or yellow onion**
- **2 cloves garlic, minced**
- **1/4 cup coarsely chopped fresh cilantro**
- **Lime wedges (optional)**

1. Cut halibut into 1-inch pieces; sprinkle with lime juice. Blend cornstarch and soy sauce in small cup until smooth. Stir in gingerroot; set aside.

2. Heat oil in wok or large nonstick skillet over medium heat until hot. Add onion and garlic; stir-fry 2 minutes. Add halibut; stir-fry 2 minutes or until fish begins to flake when tested with fork.

3. Stir soy sauce mixture; add to wok. Stir-fry 30 seconds or until sauce boils and thickens. Sprinkle with cilantro. Garnish with lime wedges. *Makes 4 servings*

Nutrients per Serving: about 1/2 cup

Calories 154	**Fiber** <1g
Fat 3g (sat <1g)	**Cholesterol** 36mg
Protein 25g	**Sodium** 592mg
Carbohydrate 5g	

Exchanges: 1 vegetable, 3 lean meat

Spinach Stuffed Manicotti

Black Bean Tostada

Black Bean Tostadas

Quick Recipe   *(Pictured above)*

    1 cup rinsed and drained canned black
        beans, mashed
    2 teaspoons chili powder
    4 (8-inch) corn tortillas
    1 cup torn romaine lettuce leaves
    1 cup chopped seeded fresh tomatoes
    1/2 cup chopped onion
    1/2 cup plain fat-free yogurt
    2 jalapeño peppers,* seeded and finely
        chopped
    Fresh cilantro sprig (optional)

*Jalapeño peppers can sting and irritate the skin, so wear
rubber gloves when handling peppers and do not touch your
eyes.*

1. Combine beans and chili powder in small
saucepan. Cook over medium heat 5 minutes
or until heated through, stirring occasionally.

2. Spray large nonstick skillet with nonstick
cooking spray. Heat over medium heat until
hot. Sprinkle tortillas with water; place in skillet,
one at a time. Cook 20 to 30 seconds or until
hot and pliable, turning once during cooking.

3. Spread bean mixture evenly over tortillas;
layer with lettuce, tomatoes, onion, yogurt and
peppers. Garnish with fresh cilantro sprig. Serve
immediately.   *Makes 4 servings*

Nutrients per Serving: 1 tostada

Calories 146	**Fiber** 5g
Fat 2g (sat <1g)	**Cholesterol** 1mg
Protein 9g	**Sodium** 466mg
Carbohydrate 29g	

Exchanges: 1-1/2 starch, 1-1/2 vegetable

Pan Seared Halibut Steaks with Avocado Salsa

Quick Recipe

    4 tablespoons chipotle salsa, divided
    1/2 teaspoon salt, divided
    4 small (4 to 5 ounces each) *or* 2 large
        (8 to 10 ounces each) halibut steaks,
        cut 3/4 inch thick
    1/2 cup diced seeded fresh tomato
    1/2 ripe avocado, diced
    2 tablespoons chopped fresh cilantro
        (optional)
    Lime wedges (optional)

1. Combine 2 tablespoons salsa and 1/4 teaspoon
salt; spread over both sides of halibut.

2. Heat large nonstick skillet over medium heat
until hot. Add halibut; cook 4 to 5 minutes per
side or until fish is opaque in center.

3. Meanwhile, combine remaining 2 tablespoons
salsa, 1/4 teaspoon salt, tomato, avocado and
cilantro, if desired, in small bowl. Spoon over
cooked fish. Garnish with lime wedges.

                    Makes 4 servings

Nutrients per Serving: 1 halibut steak with about
3 tablespoons Avocado Salsa

Calories 169	**Fiber** 4g
Fat 7g (sat <1g)	**Cholesterol** 36mg
Protein 25g	**Sodium** 476mg
Carbohydrate 2g	

Exchanges: 3 lean meat

Smoked Turkey Wrap

Smoked Turkey Wraps

low fat

(Pictured above)

Turkey Wraps

1 can (about 14 ounces) reduced-sodium chicken broth

3/4 teaspoon chopped fresh tarragon

1/2 teaspoon minced garlic

Dash black pepper

2 medium carrots, peeled and cut into 3×1/4-inch strips

1 large red bell pepper, cored, seeded and cut into 1/4-inch strips

1 medium onion, halved and thinly sliced

5 to 6 green onions or scallions, green part only, sliced in half lengthwise

Ice water

3/4 cup water

1 package (10 ounces) frozen broccoli spears, thawed

10 slices (about 1 ounce each) lean deli smoked turkey breast

Sauce

6 tablespoons no-sugar-added raspberry fruit spread

1 tablespoon plus 1 teaspoon water

1 teaspoon orange juice concentrate

1. Combine broth, tarragon, garlic and black pepper in medium saucepan; bring to a boil. Reduce heat and simmer 3 minutes.

2. Add carrots, bell pepper and onion to saucepan; cook about 7 minutes or until crisp-tender.

3. Remove vegetables with slotted spoon to small bowl; set aside.

4. Add green onions to broth and cook 1 minute or just until soft; remove and immediately drop into ice water. Pat dry with paper towels.

5. Add 3/4 cup water to remaining broth; return to a boil. Add broccoli; cook 5 minutes. Drain.

6. Take 2 green onion strips and knot ends together so total length is at least 12 inches. Repeat steps with remaining green onions until there are 5 (12-inch) strips.

7. Preheat oven to 350°F.

8. Place 2 turkey slices side by side, with long sides overlapping 1 inch, on top of 1 green onion strip. Arrange one fifth of broccoli in middle of 2 turkey slices; place one fifth of vegetable mixture on top of broccoli. Fold turkey edges together over vegetables; tie green onion into double knot. Repeat steps with remaining turkey, green onion strips and vegetables.

9. Place turkey wraps in 13×9-inch baking dish. Bake, covered, 25 to 28 minutes or until heated through.

10. Meanwhile, to make sauce, heat fruit spread, water and orange juice concentrate in small saucepan, stirring, until smooth. Spoon sauce over wraps.   *Makes 5 servings*

Nutrients per Serving: 1 wrap with about 1 tablespoon plus 1 teaspoon sauce

Calories 154	**Fiber** 3g
Fat 1g (sat <1g)	**Cholesterol** 24mg
Protein 17g	**Sodium** 738mg
Carbohydrate 19g	

Exchanges: 1/2 starch, 2 vegetable, 2 lean meat

Barley and Swiss Chard Skillet Casserole

high fiber | meatless

Quick Recipe   *(Pictured at right)*

> 1 cup water
> 3/4 cup uncooked quick-cooking barley
> 1 cup chopped red bell pepper
> 1 cup chopped green bell pepper
> 1/8 teaspoon garlic powder
> 1/8 teaspoon red pepper flakes
> 2 cups coarsely chopped packed Swiss chard leaves*
> 1 cup rinsed and drained canned reduced-sodium navy beans
> 1 cup quartered cherry tomatoes (sweet grape variety)
> 1/4 cup chopped fresh basil
> 1 tablespoon olive oil
> 2 tablespoons Italian-seasoned dry bread crumbs

Fresh spinach or beet greens can be substituted for Swiss chard.

1. Preheat broiler.

2. Bring water to a boil in large ovenproof skillet; add barley, bell peppers, garlic powder and red pepper flakes. Reduce heat; cover tightly and simmer 10 minutes or until liquid is absorbed.

3. Remove skillet from heat. Stir in chard, beans, tomatoes, basil and olive oil. Sprinkle evenly with bread crumbs. Broil, uncovered, 2 minutes or until golden.   *Makes 4 servings*

Nutrients per Serving: 1-1/4 cups casserole

Calories 288	**Fiber** 12g
Fat 6g (sat <1g)	**Cholesterol** 0mg
Protein 10g	**Sodium** 488mg
Carbohydrate 45g	

Exchanges: 2 starch, 3 vegetable, 1 fat

Chicken Roll-Ups

> 2-1/2 cups reduced-sodium marinara sauce,* divided
> 4 boneless skinless chicken breasts (about 1/4 pound each)
> 2 cups fresh baby spinach leaves
> 4 slices (1 ounce each) part-skim mozzarella cheese
> 4 tablespoons grated Parmesan cheese
> Red pepper flakes (optional)

Choose a marinara sauce with less than 800mg sodium per cup.

1. Preheat oven to 400°F. Spray 2-quart baking dish with nonstick cooking spray. Coat bottom of dish with 1 cup marinara sauce.

2. Place 1 chicken breast between 2 sheets of plastic wrap on a cutting board. Roll and pound with rolling pin until meat is about 1/4 inch thick. Repeat with remaining chicken breasts.

3. Press 1/2 cup spinach leaves onto each chicken breast. Place 1 slice mozzarella cheese on each and roll up tightly, pressing firmly. Place rolls, seam side down, in baking dish. Cover with remaining marinara sauce.

4. Cover and bake 35 minutes. Uncover and bake 10 minutes more. Top each serving with 1 tablespoon grated Parmesan cheese and red pepper flakes to taste, if desired.

Makes 4 servings

Nutrients per Serving: 1 roll-up

Calories 299	**Fiber** 3g
Fat 9g (sat 5g)	**Cholesterol** 85mg
Protein 37g	**Sodium** 782mg
Carbohydrate 16g	

Exchanges: 3 vegetable, 4-1/2 lean meat

Barley and Swiss Chard Skillet Casserole

Broccoli and Cheese Topped Potatoes

Broccoli and Cheese Topped Potatoes

meatless

Quick Recipe *(Pictured above)*

4 large baking potatoes (6 to 8 ounces each)
2 cups fresh broccoli florets
1 cup fat-free milk
1/2 cup fat-free cottage cheese
1 teaspoon dry mustard
1/2 teaspoon red pepper flakes
1 cup shredded reduced-fat sharp Cheddar cheese, divided
1 cup shredded part-skim mozzarella cheese
2 tablespoons all-purpose flour

1. Pierce potatoes several times with fork. Place in microwave oven on paper towel. Microwave on HIGH 15 minutes or just until softened. Wrap in paper towels; let stand 5 minutes.

2. Bring 4 cups water to a boil in medium saucepan over medium heat. Add broccoli. Cook 5 minutes or until broccoli is crisp-tender; drain. Add milk, cottage cheese, mustard and red pepper flakes to broccoli in saucepan; bring to a boil. Reduce heat to medium-low. Remove from heat.

3. Combine 3/4 cup Cheddar cheese, all of mozzarella cheese and flour in medium bowl. Toss to coat cheese with flour; add to broccoli mixture. Cook and stir over medium-low heat until cheese is melted and mixture is thickened.

4. Cut potatoes open. Divide broccoli mixture evenly among potatoes. Sprinkle with remaining 1/4 cup Cheddar cheese.   *Makes 4 servings*

Nutrients per Serving: 1 topped potato

Calories 381	**Fiber** 2g
Fat 9g (sat 5g)	**Cholesterol** 33mg
Protein 24g	**Sodium** 647mg
Carbohydrate 51g	

Exchanges: 3 starch, 1 vegetable, 2 lean meat, 1/2 fat

ॐ ॐ ॐ

Bolognese Sauce & Penne Pasta

cooking for 1 or 2

Quick Recipe

1/2 pound 95% lean ground beef
1/3 cup chopped onion
1 clove garlic, minced
1 can (8 ounces) tomato sauce
1/3 cup chopped carrot
1/4 cup water
2 tablespoons dry red wine
1 teaspoon dried Italian seasoning
1-1/2 cups hot cooked penne pasta
Chopped fresh parsley (optional)

1. Heat medium saucepan over medium heat until hot. Add beef, onion and garlic; cook 5 to 7 minutes or until beef is no longer pink, stirring to break up meat. Drain fat.

2. Add tomato sauce, carrot, water, wine and Italian seasoning. Bring to a boil. Reduce heat and simmer 15 minutes. Serve sauce over pasta. Sprinkle with parsley.   *Makes 2 servings*

Nutrients per Serving: 3/4 cup cooked pasta with 1/2 of sauce

Calories 292	**Fiber** 4g
Fat 5g (sat 2g)	**Cholesterol** 45mg
Protein 21g	**Sodium** 734mg
Carbohydrate 40g	

Exchanges: 2-1/2 starch, 1/2 vegetable, 2 lean meat

Chipotle Chili con Carne

(Pictured below right)

- 1 tablespoon chili powder
- 1 tablespoon ground cumin
- 3/4 pound beef stew meat, cut into 1-inch pieces
- Nonstick cooking spray
- 1 can (about 14 ounces) reduced-sodium beef broth
- 1 tablespoon minced canned chipotle chiles in adobo sauce, or to taste
- 1 can (about 14 ounces) diced tomatoes
- 1 large green bell pepper *or* 2 poblano peppers, cut into 1/2-inch pieces
- 2 cans (about 15 ounces each) pinto or red beans, rinsed and drained
- Chopped fresh cilantro (optional)

1. Combine chili powder and cumin in medium bowl. Add beef; toss to coat.

2. Coat large saucepan or Dutch oven with cooking spray; heat over medium heat. Add beef; cook and stir 5 minutes. Add beef broth and chipotles with sauce; bring to a boil. Reduce heat; cover and simmer 1 hour 15 minutes or until beef is very tender.

3. With slotted spoon, transfer beef to carving board, leaving juices in saucepan. Using 2 forks, shred beef. Return beef to saucepan; add tomatoes and bell pepper. Bring to a boil; stir in beans. Simmer, uncovered, 20 minutes or until bell pepper is tender. Garnish with cilantro. *Makes 6 servings*

Nutrients per Serving: about 1 cup chili

Calories 230	**Fiber** 10g
Fat 5g (sat 1g)	**Cholesterol** 35mg
Protein 20g	**Sodium** 679mg
Carbohydrate 27g	

Exchanges: 1-1/2 starch, 1 vegetable, 1-1/2 lean meat

Grilled Chicken with Extra Spicy Corn and Black Beans

- 3 tablespoons MRS. DASH® Extra Spicy Seasoning Blend, divided
- 1 cup canned black beans, drained and rinsed
- 1 cup frozen yellow corn, thawed, cooked and cooled
- 1 medium red bell pepper, seeded and chopped (optional)
- 1/2 cup finely chopped fresh cilantro
- 1/4 cup finely chopped red onion
- 2 tablespoons fresh lime juice
- 4 boneless skinless chicken breast halves

At least one hour before grilling chicken, to prepare Salsa, mix 2 tablespoons Mrs. Dash® Extra Spicy Seasoning Blend, black beans, yellow corn, bell pepper (if using), cilantro, red onion and fresh lime juice until well blended. Refrigerate, stirring once or twice. To prepare chicken, preheat grill to medium-high. Place 1 tablespoon Mrs. Dash® Extra Spicy Seasoning Blend and chicken in a plastic bag; shake until well coated. Grill 5 minutes. Turn and cook additional 5 minutes, or until juices run clear when chicken is pierced. Serve hot, with salsa on the side. *Makes 4 servings*

Nutrients per Serving: 1 chicken breast (about 1/4 pound uncooked weight, 3 ounces cooked) with about 1/2 cup plus 1 tablespoon salsa

Calories 220	**Fiber** 4g
Fat 2g (sat <1g)	**Cholesterol** 66mg
Protein 31g	**Sodium** 262mg
Carbohydrate 20g	

Exchanges: 1 starch, 1/2 vegetable, 4 lean meat

Chipotle Chili con Carne

Butternut Gratin

high fiber — cooking for 1 or 2

Quick Recipe   (Pictured at right)

 1 butternut squash
 6 ounces lean boneless pork chops, trimmed of fat and cooked (4 ounces cooked weight)
 1 bunch green onions, trimmed and sliced
 1/2 cup chopped celery (optional)
 1/2 cup vegetable broth
 1/3 cup whole grain bread crumbs
 2 tablespoons shredded reduced-fat Cheddar cheese
 1/4 teaspoon black pepper (optional)

Microwave Directions

1. Pierce squash with knife tip in several places. Microwave on HIGH 15 to 20 minutes or until squash is barely tender.

2. Remove squash from microwave and let rest about 5 minutes or until cool enough to handle. Cut off top and discard. Slice squash in half lengthwise and scoop out seeds. Use knife to score each half into a grid of 1-inch cubes, leaving skin intact. Then slice cubes from skin.

3. Lightly coat microwave-safe baking dish with nonstick cooking spray. Combine squash, pork, onions, celery, if desired, broth and crumbs in prepared dish. Top with cheese. Microwave on HIGH 2 to 2-1/2 minutes or until squash is tender and heated through. Season with black pepper, if desired. *Makes 2 servings*

Variation: Acorn squash can be substituted.

Note: This recipe was tested in an 1100-watt microwave oven.

Nutrients per Serving: 1/2 of total recipe

Calories 342	**Fiber** 6g
Fat 8g (sat 3g)	**Cholesterol** 83mg
Protein 33g	**Sodium** 388mg
Carbohydrate 37g	

Exchanges: 1 starch, 4-1/2 vegetable, 3 lean meat

Shell Pasta with Ham and Peas

Quick Recipe

 2 cups (about 6 ounces) uncooked medium shell pasta
 6 ounces cooked 96% fat-free ham
1-1/4 cups 2% milk
 1 to 1-1/2 cups frozen peas
 2 cloves garlic, minced
1-1/2 teaspoons dried basil
 1/4 teaspoon red pepper flakes *or* 1/8 teaspoon ground red pepper (cayenne)
 1/4 cup reduced-fat cream cheese
 2 tablespoons freshly grated Parmesan cheese

1. Cook pasta according to package directions, omitting salt. Drain and rinse well under cold water until pasta is cool; drain well.

2. Cut ham into 1/4-inch strips; set aside.

3. Combine milk, peas, garlic, basil and red pepper flakes in large nonstick skillet. Bring to a boil over medium heat. Reduce heat to low; simmer, uncovered, 5 minutes.

4. Add cream cheese to skillet; gently stir until blended. Add ham and pasta. Cook over medium heat until heated through. Sprinkle with Parmesan cheese just before serving. *Makes 4 servings*

Nutrients per Serving: about 1 cup

Calories 295	**Fiber** 3g
Fat 8g (sat 4g)	**Cholesterol** 32mg
Protein 21g	**Sodium** 706mg
Carbohydrate 33g	

Exchanges: 2 starch, 2 lean meat, 1/2 fat

Lemon Salmon and Spinach Pasta

Lemon Salmon and Spinach Pasta

low sodium

Quick Recipe   (Pictured above)

3/4 pound salmon fillet
8 ounces uncooked fettuccine
4 teaspoons butter
1 teaspoon finely grated lemon peel
2 cloves garlic, minced
1/4 teaspoon red pepper flakes
2 tablespoons lemon juice
3 cups baby spinach leaves
1/2 cup shredded peeled carrots

1. Pat salmon dry with paper towels. Remove skin from salmon; discard. Cut fish into 1/2-inch pieces.

2. Cook fettuccine according to package directions, omitting salt. Drain and return to hot saucepan.

3. Meanwhile, melt butter in large skillet over medium-high heat. Add salmon, lemon peel, garlic and red pepper flakes; cook 4 to 7 minutes or until salmon begins to flake when tested with fork. Gently stir in lemon juice.

4. Add salmon mixture, spinach and carrots to hot cooked fettuccine; gently toss to combine. Serve immediately.   *Makes 4 servings*

Nutrients per Serving: 1-1/2 cups

Calories 410	**Fiber** 4g
Fat 14g (sat 5g)	**Cholesterol** 53mg
Protein 25g	**Sodium** 107mg
Carbohydrate 45g	

Exchanges: 3 starch, 2 lean meat, 1-1/2 fat

Chiles Rellenos Casserole

 low carb

4 small tomatoes (about 1 pound), peeled
1 small white onion, peeled and quartered
1 clove garlic
1 tablespoon light olive or canola oil
1/2 cup reduced-sodium chicken broth
1/4 cup canned chopped mild green chiles
    Pinch ground cloves
    Pinch ground cinnamon
6 canned whole mild green chiles
4 ounces reduced-fat Monterey Jack
    cheese, cut into 6 sticks
2 eggs and 2 egg whites *or* 1/2 cup plus
    2 tablespoons egg substitute, lightly
    beaten

1. Combine tomatoes, onion and garlic in blender or food processor container; purée. Heat oil in medium saucepan over medium-low heat. Add tomato mixture; cook 10 minutes. Add broth, chopped chiles, cloves and cinnamon. Cover and simmer gently 15 minutes. Keep warm until ready for use.

2. Preheat oven to 350°F. Lightly spray 13×9-inch baking dish with nonstick cooking spray.

3. Cut slit in side of each whole chile; remove as many seeds as possible. Pat dry. Place 1 cheese stick in each chile. Place stuffed chiles in single layer in prepared dish. Pour beaten eggs over chiles.

4. Bake about 25 to 30 minutes or until eggs are set and casserole browns and puffs. Cut lengthwise into 6 slices, each containing 1 whole stuffed chile. Top each serving with warm tomato salsa. *Makes 6 servings*

Nutrients per Serving: 1 stuffed chile with about 1/3 cup salsa

Calories 133	**Fiber** 2g
Fat 8g (sat <g)	**Cholesterol** mg
Protein 9g	**Sodium** 941mg
Carbohydrate 6g	

Exchanges: 1 vegetable, 1 lean meat, 1 fat

Turkey Jambalaya

Quick Recipe

1 teaspoon canola oil
1 cup chopped onion
1 medium green bell pepper, cored,
    seeded and chopped
1/2 cup chopped celery
3 cloves garlic, finely chopped
1-3/4 cups reduced-sodium chicken broth
1 cup chopped seeded fresh tomato
6 ounces 93% lean ground turkey
6 ounces lean turkey sausage
3 tablespoons tomato paste
1 bay leaf
1 teaspoon dried basil
1/4 teaspoon ground red pepper (cayenne)
1 cup uncooked white rice
1/4 cup chopped fresh parsley

1. Heat oil in large nonstick skillet over medium-high heat until hot. Add onion, bell pepper, celery and garlic. Cook and stir 5 minutes or until vegetables are tender.

2. Add chicken broth, tomato, turkey, turkey sausage, tomato paste, bay leaf, basil and red pepper. Stir in rice. Bring to a boil over high heat, stirring occasionally. Reduce heat to medium-low. Simmer, covered, 20 minutes or until rice is tender.

3. Remove skillet from heat. Remove and discard bay leaf. Top individual servings with parsley. Serve immediately.

Makes 4 servings

Nutrients per Serving: 1 cup jambalaya

Calories 358	**Fiber** 3g
Fat 8g (sat 2g)	**Cholesterol** 57mg
Protein 23g	**Sodium** 558mg
Carbohydrate 49g	

Exchanges: 2-1/2 starch, 2-1/2 vegetable, 1-1/2 lean meat

Curried Chicken & Vegetables with Rice

Quick Recipe

> 1 pound boneless skinless chicken breasts or breast tenders, cut into 1/2-inch slices
> 2 teaspoons curry powder
> 1/4 teaspoon salt
> 1/4 teaspoon ground red pepper (cayenne)
> 1 tablespoon canola oil
> 1 medium onion, chopped
> 3 cloves garlic, minced
> 1-1/4 cups reduced-sodium chicken broth, divided
> 1 package (16 ounces) frozen mixed vegetables (broccoli, bell peppers, cauliflower, sugar snap peas), thawed
> 2 tablespoons tomato paste
> 2 teaspoons cornstarch
> 3 cups hot cooked white rice
> 1/2 cup plain fat-free yogurt
> 1/3 cup chopped fresh cilantro

1. Toss chicken with curry powder, salt and ground red pepper in medium bowl. Heat oil in large skillet over medium heat. Add onion; cook 5 minutes, stirring occasionally. Add chicken and garlic; cook 4 minutes or until chicken is no longer pink, stirring occasionally. Add 1 cup chicken broth, vegetables and tomato paste; bring to a boil over high heat. Reduce heat to medium; simmer, uncovered, 3 to 4 minutes or until vegetables are crisp-tender.

2. Mix cornstarch and remaining 1/4 cup chicken broth until smooth. Stir into chicken mixture. Bring to a boil; cook and stir 2 minutes or until sauce thickens. Serve over rice; top with yogurt and cilantro. *Makes 6 servings*

Nutrients per Serving: 1 cup chicken mixture with 1/2 cup cooked rice, 4 teaspoons yogurt and about 2-1/2 teaspoons cilantro

Calories 269	**Fiber** 3g
Fat 5g (sat 1g)	**Cholesterol** 46mg
Protein 23g	**Sodium** 199mg
Carbohydrate 33g	

Exchanges: 1-1/2 starch, 2 vegetable, 2 lean meat

Spinach Crêpes

> 2 cups egg substitute
> 1 cup reduced-sodium chicken broth, divided
> 1 tablespoon all-purpose flour
> 1-1/4 cups shredded reduced-fat Swiss cheese
> 1/2 teaspoon white pepper
> 1/2 teaspoon ground nutmeg
> 1 package (10 ounces) frozen chopped spinach, thawed and squeezed dry
> 1 can (8 ounces) reduced-sodium tomato sauce

1. Preheat oven to 375°F. Spray 10-inch nonstick skillet with nonstick cooking spray; heat over medium-high heat. Pour in 1/4 cup egg substitute, tilting pan to coat surface. Cook about 1 minute or until lightly browned and set. Flip crêpe; cook about 15 seconds. Slide crêpe onto dinner plate and cover with waxed paper. Repeat, spraying skillet as needed, until 8 crêpes are cooked and stacked with waxed paper.

2. Combine chicken broth and flour in large saucepan, stirring until smooth. Bring to a boil. Reduce heat; cook and stir 2 minutes or until thick. Add cheese, pepper and nutmeg; cook, stirring, until cheese melts. Stir spinach into cheese mixture.

3. Spray 13×9-inch baking dish with cooking spray; set aside.

4. With browned side of crêpe down, spread 3 tablespoons filling onto one third of crêpe; roll up. Place rolled crêpe in prepared baking dish. Repeat with remaining crêpes and filling.

5. Spread tomato sauce over crêpes. Bake at 375°F 25 to 30 minutes. *Makes 4 servings*

Nutrients per Serving: 2 crêpes

Calories 218	**Fiber** 3g
Fat 7g (sat 2g)	**Cholesterol** 13mg
Protein 29g	**Sodium** 507mg
Carbohydrate 11g	

Exchanges: 1/2 starch, 1 vegetable, 3-1/2 lean meat

Curried Chicken & Vegetables with Rice

Cheesy Polenta with Zucchini Stew

Cheesy Polenta with Zucchini Stew

meatless

(Pictured above)

2-1/4 cups water, divided
1 cup stone-ground or regular yellow cornmeal
2 eggs
2 egg whites
3/4 cup shredded reduced-fat sharp Cheddar cheese
1 jalapeño pepper,* minced
1 teaspoon butter
1/2 teaspoon salt, divided
1 tablespoon olive oil
2 cups coarsely chopped eggplant
1 cup chopped onion
3 cloves garlic, minced
3 cups chopped zucchini
1 cup chopped seeded fresh tomato
1/2 cup chopped yellow bell pepper
2 tablespoons minced fresh parsley
1 tablespoon minced fresh oregano
1/4 teaspoon minced fresh rosemary
1/4 teaspoon red pepper flakes
1/4 teaspoon ground pepper blend

Jalapeño peppers can sting and irritate the skin, so wear rubber gloves when handling peppers and do not touch your eyes.

1. Bring 2 cups water to a boil. Slowly add cornmeal, stirring constantly. Bring to a boil, stirring constantly, until mixture thickens.

2. Lightly beat eggs and egg whites with remaining 1/4 cup water. Add to cornmeal; cook and stir until bubbly. Remove from heat; stir in cheese, jalapeño pepper, butter and 1/4 teaspoon salt. Pour into 9-inch square baking pan. Cover and refrigerate several hours or until firm.

3. Heat olive oil in medium saucepan over medium heat until hot. Cook and stir eggplant, onion and garlic 5 minutes or until onion is transparent. Add zucchini, tomato, bell pepper, parsley, oregano, rosemary, remaining 1/4 teaspoon salt, red pepper flakes and pepper blend. Simmer, uncovered, 1 hour.

4. Spray large nonstick skillet with nonstick cooking spray. Heat over medium heat until hot. Cut polenta into 6 rectangles. Cook over medium heat 8 minutes per side or until crusty and lightly browned. Serve zucchini stew over polenta. *Makes 6 servings*

Nutrients per Serving: 1 polenta rectangle with 3/4 cup vegetable mixture

Calories 219	**Fiber** 3g
Fat 7g (sat 2g)	**Cholesterol** 82mg
Protein 10g	**Sodium** 435mg
Carbohydrate 29g	

Exchanges: 1-1/2 starch, 1 vegetable, 1 lean meat, 1/2 fat

Tip

Eggplant, the large, pear-shaped fruit with smooth, glossy, dark purple skin becomes bitter with age. Its skin, perfectly edible when the eggplant is young, should be removed from older fruit.

Pork and Toasted Peanut Toss

Quick Recipe

1 bag boil-in-bag rice *or* 1 cup uncooked instant rice

1/4 cup plus 2 tablespoons unsalted dry-roasted peanuts

Nonstick cooking spray

1/2 pound boneless pork tenderloin, trimmed of fat and cut into thin strips

3 tablespoons cider vinegar

3 tablespoons reduced-sodium soy sauce

2 tablespoons water

4 packets sugar substitute*

2 teaspoons grated fresh gingerroot

1/8 teaspoon salt

1/8 teaspoon red pepper flakes

1 medium onion, cut into 8 wedges

1 large green bell pepper, cored, seeded and thinly sliced

1 medium carrot, cut into 1/8×2-inch strips

This recipe was tested with sucralose-based sugar substitute.

1. Cook rice according to package directions, omitting salt; set aside.

2. Heat medium skillet over medium-high heat. Add peanuts; cook, stirring constantly, 3 minutes or until peanuts are lightly browned. Remove from skillet; set aside.

3. Spray same skillet with cooking spray. Add pork; cook, stirring constantly, 3 minutes or until no longer pink. Remove from skillet; set aside.

4. Meanwhile, combine vinegar, soy sauce, water, sugar substitute, gingerroot, salt and red pepper flakes in small saucepan; stir until well blended. Heat over medium heat until warm.

5. Spray skillet with cooking spray. Add vegetables; coat vegetables with cooking spray. Cook, stirring frequently, 4 minutes or until crisp-tender. Add pork and peanuts to skillet; cook and stir 30 seconds to reheat.

6. Serve pork mixture over rice. Spoon sauce over top. *Makes 4 servings*

Nutrients per Serving: 1 cup pork mixture with 1/2 cup cooked long-grain white rice

Calories 285	**Fiber** 3g
Fat 9g (sat 2g)	**Cholesterol** 37mg
Protein 19g	**Sodium** 495mg
Carbohydrate 34g	

Exchanges: 2 starch, 1 vegetable, 1-1/2 lean meat, 1/2 fat

ैa ैa ैa

Light Creamed Turkey and Baked Potatoes

Quick Recipe

1 package JENNIE-O TURKEY STORE® Turkey Breast Slices

2 tablespoons margarine or butter

2 tablespoons all-purpose flour

1-2/3 cups skim or low-fat milk

1 cup frozen peas, thawed

1 jar (2 ounces) diced pimiento, drained

1/2 teaspoon poultry seasoning

Salt and pepper (optional)

4 hot baked potatoes

Cut across grain of turkey slices to make strips 1/2 inch wide and 2-1/2 inches long. In large skillet over medium heat, melt margarine. Cook and stir turkey until no longer pink, about 4 minutes. Sprinkle flour over turkey; cook and stir 2 minutes. Stir in milk and cook until thickened, about 3 minutes. Stir in peas, pimiento, poultry seasoning and salt and pepper to taste. Serve over split baked potatoes. *Makes 4 servings*

Nutrients per Serving: 1 medium-sized baked potato with 1 cup turkey mixture (without salt and pepper seasoning)

Calories 412	**Fiber** 5g
Fat 8g (sat 1g)	**Cholesterol** 53mg
Protein 39g	**Sodium** 238mg
Carbohydrate 48g	

Exchanges: 3 starch, 1/2 milk, 3-1/2 lean meat

Tomato, Potato and Basil Skillet

meatless

Quick Recipe   *(Pictured at right)*

    1 tablespoon olive oil, divided
    3 cups sliced potatoes
 1/3 cup minced fresh basil
    2 whole eggs
    2 egg whites
    2 tablespoons fat-free milk
    1 tablespoon Dijon mustard
    1 teaspoon dry mustard
 1/2 teaspoon salt
 1/4 teaspoon black pepper
    2 cups sliced plum tomatoes

1. Heat 1-1/2 teaspoons oil in medium nonstick skillet over medium heat until hot. Layer half of potato slices in skillet. Cover and cook 3 minutes or until lightly browned.

2. Turn potatoes; cook, covered, 3 minutes or until lightly browned.

3. Remove potatoes from skillet. Repeat with remaining 1-1/2 teaspoons oil and potatoes.

4. Arrange all potatoes in skillet. Sprinkle with basil.

5. Whisk together eggs, egg whites, milk, Dijon, dry mustard, salt and pepper in small bowl. Pour over potatoes. Arrange tomatoes over potato mixture.

6. Reduce heat to low. Cover and cook 10 minutes or until eggs are set. Cut into 4 wedges to serve.   *Makes 4 servings*

Nutrients per Serving: 1 skillet wedge

Calories 210	**Fiber** 4g
Fat 7g (sat 1g)	**Cholesterol** 106mg
Protein 9g	**Sodium** 473mg
Carbohydrate 29g	

Exchanges: 1-1/2 starch, 1 vegetable, 1/2 lean meat, 1 fat

Creole Shrimp and Rice

Quick Recipe

    2 tablespoons olive oil
    1 cup uncooked rice
    1 can (about 14 ounces) diced tomatoes with garlic
1-1/2 cups water
    1 teaspoon Creole or Cajun seasoning blend
    1 pound medium cooked shrimp, peeled
    1 package (10 ounces) frozen okra *or* 1-1/2 cups frozen sugar snap peas, thawed

1. Heat oil in large skillet over medium heat until hot. Add rice; cook and stir 2 to 3 minutes or until lightly browned.

2. Add tomatoes, water and seasoning blend; bring to a boil. Reduce heat; cover and simmer 15 minutes.

3. Add shrimp and okra. Cook, covered, 3 minutes or until heated through.
         Makes 4 servings

Nutrients per Serving: 1-3/4 cups

Calories 406	**Fiber** 3g
Fat 8g (sat 1g)	**Cholesterol** 221mg
Protein 30g	**Sodium** 831mg
Carbohydrate 51g	

Exchanges: 3 starch, 1 vegetable, 3 lean meat

Penne with Roasted Tomato Sauce and Mozzarella

high fiber

- 1/4 teaspoon olive oil
- 3 cloves garlic, minced
- 2 cans (28 ounces each) fire-roasted or regular diced tomatoes
- 1/4 teaspoon black pepper
- 2-1/2 cups (8-1/2 ounces) uncooked penne pasta
- 3/4 pound reduced-fat smoked turkey sausage, cut into 1/4-inch-thick slices
- 1 cup part-skim mozzarella cheese, cut into 1/4-inch cubes, at room temperature
- 1/4 cup chopped fresh basil

1. Heat oil in large saucepan over medium-high heat until hot. Add garlic; cook and stir 2 minutes. Add tomatoes and pepper. Bring to a boil. Reduce heat. Cover; simmer 15 minutes. Cool slightly.

2. Meanwhile, cook pasta according to package directions, omitting salt; drain. Set aside; keep warm.

3. Place half of tomatoes in blender or food processor container; blend just until coarsely chopped. Add tomato purée to pasta; toss to combine.

4. Heat small nonstick skillet over medium-high heat. Add sausage; cook and stir 3 minutes. Remove sausage to large saucepan with remaining tomato mixture. Cover; simmer over medium heat 5 minutes or until heated through.

5. Add pasta to saucepan; toss to combine. Stir in cheese, basil and salt, if desired. Serve immediately.   *Makes 6 servings*

Note: This recipe makes about 3 cups of sauce. The tomato sauce would be good with any kind of pasta. You could also substitute fresh parsley for the basil.

Nutrients per Serving: about 1 cup

Calories 296	Fiber 5g
Fat 6g (sat 3g)	Cholesterol 32mg
Protein 19g	Sodium 934mg
Carbohydrate 42g	

Exchanges: 2 starch, 2 vegetable, 1-1/2 lean meat

Barley Beef Stroganoff

high fiber

- 1-1/2 cups vegetable broth
- 1 cup water
- 2/3 cup uncooked pearl barley (not quick-cooking)
- 1 package (6 ounces) sliced fresh mushrooms
- 1/2 teaspoon dried marjoram
- 1/2 teaspoon black pepper
- 1/2 pound 95% lean ground beef
- 1/2 cup chopped celery
- 1/2 cup minced green onions
- 1/4 cup fat-free half-and-half
  Minced fresh parsley (optional)

Slow Cooker Directions

1. Place broth, water, barley, mushrooms, marjoram and pepper in 3-quart slow cooker. Cover; cook on LOW 6 to 7 hours.

2. Brown beef in large nonstick skillet over medium-high heat 6 to 8 minutes, stirring to break up meat. Drain fat. Add celery and green onions; cook and stir 3 minutes. Stir beef mixture and half-and-half into slow cooker mixture. Cover; cook on HIGH 10 to 15 minutes or until beef is hot and vegetables are tender. Garnish with parsley.   *Makes 4 servings*

Nutrients per Serving: 1-1/4 cups stroganoff

Calories 228	Fiber 6g
Fat 4g (sat 2g)	Cholesterol 36mg
Protein 18g	Sodium 453mg
Carbohydrate 31g	

Exchanges: 2 starch, 1/2 vegetable, 2 lean meat

Stuffed Pork Tenderloin

Stuffed Pork Tenderloin

(Pictured above)

1/3 cup chopped onion

1 clove garlic, minced

1 tablespoon stick butter or margarine

1 small tart apple, peeled, cored and finely chopped

1/4 cup chopped pitted prunes

1/4 cup dry white wine or unsweetened apple juice

2 tablespoons EQUAL® SPOONFUL*

3/4 teaspoon dried rosemary leaves

3/4 teaspoon dried thyme leaves

1/4 cup cornbread stuffing crumbs

Salt and pepper (optional)

1 whole pork tenderloin (about 16 ounces)

1 clove garlic, minced

*May substitute 3 packets EQUAL® sweetener.

• Sauté onion and 1 clove garlic in butter in medium skillet until tender, about 5 minutes. Add apple and prunes; cook 2 to 3 minutes. Add wine, Equal® and 1/2 teaspoon each rosemary and thyme; cook, covered, over medium heat about 5 minutes or until wine is evaporated. Stir in stuffing crumbs; season to taste with salt and pepper.

• Cut lengthwise slit about 2 inches deep in pork tenderloin. Mix remaining rosemary, thyme and 1 clove garlic; rub over outside surface of pork. Spoon fruit stuffing into pork and place in baking pan.

• Roast meat, uncovered, in preheated 350°F oven about 45 minutes (meat thermometer will register 160°F) or until no longer pink in center. Let stand 5 to 10 minutes before slicing.

Makes 4 servings

Tip: The stuffing can also be used to stuff lean pork chops. Cut pockets in chops with a sharp knife, or have a butcher cut the pockets for you.

Nutrients per Serving: about 3 ounces pork (cooked weight) with 1/4 cup fruit stuffing (without salt and pepper seasoning)

Calories 243		**Fiber** 2g
Fat 7g (sat 3g)		**Cholesterol** 74mg
Protein 25g		**Sodium** 117mg
Carbohydrate 18g		

Exchanges: 1 fruit, 3 lean meat

Tip

When shopping for prunes, choose fruit that is somewhat soft. The skin should be bluish black and free of blemishes. If kept in a cool, dry place, prunes will keep for up to six months. Refrigerated, they last nine months, and they can be frozen for up to a year.

Sides & Salads

ॐ ॐ ॐ

Chicken and Spinach Salad

Quick Recipe   *(Pictured at left)*

3/4 **pound chicken breast tenders**
   Nonstick cooking spray
4 **cups washed, stemmed and torn spinach**
2 **cups torn romaine lettuce**
1 **large grapefruit, peeled and sectioned**
8 **thin slices red onion, separated into rings**
2 **tablespoons crumbled blue cheese**
1/2 **cup frozen citrus blend concentrate, thawed**
1/4 **cup fat-free Italian salad dressing**
   Assorted fresh greens (optional)

1. Cut chicken into 2×1/2-inch strips. Spray large nonstick skillet with cooking spray; heat over medium heat until hot. Add chicken; cook and stir 5 minutes or until no longer pink. Remove from skillet; set aside.

2. Divide spinach, lettuce, grapefruit, onion, cheese and chicken among 4 salad plates. Combine citrus blend concentrate and Italian dressing in small bowl; drizzle over salads. Garnish with assorted greens.   *Makes 4 servings*

Nutrients per Serving: 2 cups salad

Calories 218	**Fiber** 3g
Fat 4g (sat 1g)	**Cholesterol** 55mg
Protein 23g	**Sodium** 361mg
Carbohydrate 23g	

Exchanges: 1 fruit, 2 vegetable, 2-1/2 lean meat

Clockwise from top left: Zesty Taco Salad (page 108), Polenta Triangles (page 117), Chicken and Spinach Salad and Potato-Cabbage Pancakes (page 111)

Southwestern Bean and Corn Salad

1 can (about 15 ounces) pinto beans, rinsed and drained

1 cup fresh corn kernels (about 2 ears) or thawed frozen corn

1 medium red bell pepper, cored, seeded and finely chopped

4 green onions, finely chopped

2 tablespoons cider vinegar

2 tablespoons honey

1/2 teaspoon salt

1/2 teaspoon ground mustard

1/2 teaspoon ground cumin

1/8 teaspoon ground red pepper (cayenne)

Fresh lettuce leaves (optional)

1. Combine beans, corn, bell pepper and onions in large bowl.

2. Blend vinegar and honey in small bowl until smooth. Stir in salt, mustard, cumin and red pepper. Drizzle over bean mixture; toss to coat. Cover; refrigerate 2 hours. Serve on lettuce leaves, if desired. *Makes 4 servings*

Note: Canned beans are high in sodium. Researchers have found, however, that rinsing the beans under running water for 1 minute eliminates up to 40 percent of the sodium.

Nutrients per Serving: about 3/4 cup salad

Calories 163	**Fiber** 1g
Fat 1g (sat <1g)	**Cholesterol** 0mg
Protein 7g	**Sodium** 608mg
Carbohydrate 36g	

Exchanges: 2 starch, 1 vegetable

Braised Oriental Cabbage

Quick Recipe

1 small head bok choy (about 3/4 pound)

1/2 small head green cabbage (about 1/2 pound)

1/2 cup reduced-sodium chicken broth

2 tablespoons rice wine vinegar

2 tablespoons reduced-sodium soy sauce

1 tablespoon brown sugar

1/4 teaspoon red pepper flakes (optional)

1 tablespoon cornstarch

1 tablespoon water

1. Trim and discard bottoms from bok choy; slice stems into 1/2-inch pieces. Cut tops of leaves into 1/2-inch slices; set aside. Cut cabbage into 1-inch pieces.

2. Combine bok choy stems and cabbage in large nonstick skillet. Add broth, vinegar, soy sauce, brown sugar and red pepper flakes, if desired. Bring to a boil over high heat. Reduce heat to medium. Cover and simmer 5 minutes or until vegetables are crisp-tender.

3. Blend cornstarch and water in small bowl until smooth. Stir into skillet. Cook and stir 1 minute or until sauce boils and thickens.

4. Stir in reserved bok choy leaves; cook 1 minute. *Makes 6 servings*

Nutrients per Serving: 3/4 cup

Calories 34	**Fiber** 1g
Fat <1g (sat <1g)	**Cholesterol** 0mg
Protein 2g	**Sodium** 170mg
Carbohydrate 6g	

Exchanges: 1-1/2 vegetable

Southwestern Bean and Corn Salad

Zesty Taco Salad

(Pictured on page 104)

high fiber

2 tablespoons canola oil

1 clove garlic, finely chopped

3/4 pound 93% lean ground turkey

1-3/4 teaspoons chili powder

1/4 teaspoon ground cumin

3 cups torn lettuce

1 can (about 14 ounces) Mexican-style diced tomatoes, drained

1 cup rinsed and drained canned chickpeas or pinto beans

2/3 cup chopped peeled cucumber

1/3 cup frozen corn, thawed

1/4 cup chopped red onion

1 to 2 jalapeño peppers,* seeded and finely chopped (optional)

1 tablespoon red wine vinegar

12 baked tortilla chips

Fresh greens and fresh cilantro (optional)

Jalapeño peppers can sting and irritate the skin, so wear rubber gloves when handling peppers and do not touch your eyes.

1. Combine oil and garlic in small bowl; let stand 1 hour at room temperature.

2. Combine turkey, chili powder and cumin in large nonstick skillet. Cook over medium heat 5 minutes or until turkey is no longer pink, stirring to crumble.

3. Combine turkey, lettuce, tomatoes, chickpeas, cucumber, corn, onion and jalapeño pepper, if desired, in large bowl. Remove garlic from oil; discard garlic. Add vinegar to oil. Drizzle over salad; toss to coat. Serve salad on tortilla chips and fresh greens, if desired. Garnish with cilantro. *Makes 4 servings*

Nutrients per Serving: 1-1/2 cups salad with 3 tortilla chips

Calories 285	**Fiber** 5g
Fat 11g (sat 1g)	**Cholesterol** 33mg
Protein 21g	**Sodium** 484mg
Carbohydrate 28g	

Exchanges: 1-1/2 starch, 1 vegetable, 2 lean meat, 1 fat

Brussels Sprouts with Walnuts

high fiber **meatless**

1 pound brussels sprouts, trimmed

2 cups water

1 cup apple juice

1 cup butternut squash, diced into 1-inch cubes

1/2 cup fat-free vinaigrette salad dressing

1 cup arugula, mixed baby lettuce or baby spinach leaves

1/2 cup chopped walnuts, toasted*

To toast walnuts, spread in a single layer on baking sheet. Bake in preheated 350°F oven 8 to 10 minutes or until golden brown, stirring frequently.

1. Combine sprouts, water and apple juice in medium saucepan. Simmer over medium heat about 15 minutes or until sprouts are tender. Rinse under cool water and drain well.

2. Preheat oven to 400°F. Lightly coat baking sheet with nonstick cooking spray. Roast squash on baking sheet 20 minutes or until tender. Remove from oven; let cool 5 minutes.

3. When cool enough to handle, slice sprouts lengthwise into thin slices. Mix with warm squash. Toss with fat-free dressing.

4. Divide greens among 4 serving plates. Spoon vegetables over greens and sprinkle with walnuts. *Makes 4 servings*

Nutrients per Serving: 1 cup

Calories 190	**Fiber** 6g
Fat 10g (sat 1g)	**Cholesterol** 0mg
Protein 7g	**Sodium** 204mg
Carbohydrate 20g	

Exchanges: 1-1/2 starch, 2 fat

Tip

Brussels sprouts are done cooking when they've reached an intense, bright-green color and a metal skewer or fork can be easily inserted into their stem end.

Fruited Berry Squares

- 1 cup water
- 1 package (4-serving size) sugar-free berry- or berry-and-fruit-flavored gelatin
- 1 cup sliced frozen strawberries
- 1 cup frozen blueberries
- 2 ounces reduced-fat cream cheese
- 1/4 cup fat-free sour cream
- 1/4 cup fat-free half-and-half
- 2 packets sugar substitute*
- 1/4 teaspoon ground cinnamon
- 1/8 teaspoon almond extract
- Fresh lettuce leaves (optional)

This recipe was tested with sucralose-based sugar substitute.

1. Bring water to a boil in medium saucepan over high heat. Remove from heat. Add gelatin; stir until completely dissolved. Stir in frozen berries.

2. Pour gelatin mixture into 8-inch square glass dish or nonstick baking pan.** Cover with plastic wrap; refrigerate until firm.

3. Meanwhile, combine remaining ingredients except lettuce leaves in small mixing bowl; whisk until smooth. Cover; refrigerate.

4. When gelatin mixture is firm, spoon cream cheese mixture evenly over top. Serve on bed of fresh lettuce leaves. *Makes 4 servings*

**Or, the gelatin mixture can also be poured into 4 (4-ounce) glass dishes, if desired.*

Nutrients per Serving: 1/2 cup gelatin with 3 tablespoons cream cheese mixture

Calories 105	**Fiber** 2g
Fat 3g (sat 2g)	**Cholesterol** 10mg
Protein 4g	**Sodium** 121mg
Carbohydrate 14g	

Exchanges: 1 fruit, 1/2 lean meat, 1/2 fat

Oven "Fries"

(Pictured below)

- 2 small baking potatoes (about 5 ounces each)
- 2 teaspoons olive oil
- 1/4 teaspoon salt or onion salt

1. Place potatoes in refrigerator for 1 to 2 days.

2. Preheat oven to 450°F. Peel potatoes and cut lengthwise into 1/4-inch-square strips. Place in colander. Rinse potato strips under cold running water 2 minutes. Drain. Pat dry with paper towels. Place potatoes in small resealable plastic bag. Drizzle with oil. Seal bag; shake to coat potatoes with oil.

3. Arrange potatoes in single layer on baking sheet. Bake 20 to 25 minutes or until light brown and crisp. Sprinkle with salt or onion salt. *Makes 2 servings*

Note: Refrigerating potatoes—not usually recommended—converts starch in the potatoes to sugar, which enhances browning when the potatoes are baked. Do not refrigerate the potatoes longer than 2 days, or they might begin to taste sweet.

Nutrients per Serving: 1/2 of fries

Calories 172	**Fiber** 3g
Fat 5g (sat 1g)	**Cholesterol** 0mg
Protein 4g	**Sodium** 309mg
Carbohydrate 30g	

Exchanges: 2 starch, 1 fat

Oven "Fries"

3. Add broth, gingerroot and remaining 4 teaspoons teriyaki sauce to skillet. Bring to a boil over high heat. Reduce heat to medium. Add noodles; heat through. Add omelet strips and onions; heat through. Sprinkle with remaining 2 teaspoons sesame seeds.

Makes 4 servings

Nutrients per Serving: about 3/4 cup

Calories 111	**Fiber** <1g
Fat 2g (sat 1g)	**Cholesterol** 0mg
Protein 7g	**Sodium** 226mg
Carbohydrate 16g	

Exchanges: 1 starch, 1/2 lean meat, 1/2 fat

Boston Baked Beans

low fat

> 2 cans (about 15 ounces each) Great Northern or navy beans, rinsed and drained
> 1/2 cup beer (not dark beer)
> 1/3 cup finely chopped red or yellow onion
> 1/3 cup ketchup
> 3 tablespoons light molasses
> 2 teaspoons Worcestershire sauce
> 1 teaspoon dry mustard
> 1/2 teaspoon ground ginger
> 4 slices bacon (about 1 ounce each)

1. Preheat oven to 350°F. Place beans in 11×7-inch glass baking dish. Combine beer, onion, ketchup, molasses, Worcestershire sauce, mustard and ginger in medium bowl. Pour over beans; toss to coat.

2. Cut bacon into 1-inch pieces; arrange in single layer over beans. Bake, uncovered, 40 to 45 minutes or until most liquid is absorbed and bacon is browned.   *Makes 6 servings*

Nutrients per Serving: about 1/3 cup

Calories 239	**Fiber** <1g
Fat 3g (sat 1g)	**Cholesterol** 7mg
Protein 13g	**Sodium** 971mg
Carbohydrate 41g	

Exchanges: 2-1/2 starch, 1 lean meat

Ginger Noodles with Sesame Egg Strips

Ginger Noodles with Sesame Egg Strips

low fat

Quick Recipe   (Pictured above)

> 5 egg whites
> 6 teaspoons teriyaki sauce, divided
> 3 teaspoons toasted sesame seeds,* divided
> 1 teaspoon dark sesame oil
> 1/2 cup reduced-sodium chicken broth
> 1 tablespoon minced fresh gingerroot
> 6 ounces Chinese rice noodles or vermicelli, cooked and well drained
> 1/3 cup sliced green onions

*To toast sesame seeds, spread seeds in small skillet. Shake skillet over medium heat 2 minutes or until seeds begin to pop and turn golden.

1. Beat together egg whites, 2 teaspoons teriyaki sauce and 1 teaspoon sesame seeds.

2. Heat large nonstick skillet over medium heat. Add oil; heat until hot. Pour egg mixture into skillet; cook 1-1/2 to 2 minutes or until bottom of omelet is set. Turn omelet over; cook 30 seconds to 1 minute. Slide out onto plate; cool and cut into 1/2-inch strips.

Potato-Cabbage Pancakes

Quick Recipe   (Pictured on page 104)

1 cup refrigerated no-added-fat shredded hash brown potatoes

1 cup coleslaw mix, lightly packed

1/2 cup egg substitute

1/2 teaspoon white pepper

8 tablespoons unsweetened applesauce (optional)

4 tablespoons fat-free sour cream (optional)

1. Combine potatoes, coleslaw mix, egg whites and pepper in medium bowl. Spray large nonstick skillet with nonstick cooking spray. Heat over medium-high heat until hot. Drop potato mixture into skillet by 1/2-cupfuls. Repeat with second pancake. Drizzle any juices from bowl over pancakes.

2. When batter begins to sizzle, gently press down with spatula to flatten into pancakes that are 1/2 inch thick and about 4 inches in diameter. Cook 2 pancakes at a time, 4 to 5 minutes per side or until pancake browns on both sides.

3. Top each pancake with either 2 tablespoons applesauce or 1 tablespoon sour cream, if desired.   *Makes 4 servings*

Nutrients per Serving: 1 pancake

Calories 82	**Fiber** 2g
Fat 0g (sat 0g)	**Cholesterol** 0mg
Protein 5g	**Sodium** 74mg
Carbohydrate 17g	

Exchanges: 1 starch

Green Chili Rice

Quick Recipe   (Pictured below)

1 can (about 14 ounces) reduced-sodium chicken broth plus water to measure 2 cups

1 cup uncooked white rice

1 can (4 ounces) diced mild green chiles

1/2 medium yellow onion, peeled and diced

1 teaspoon dried oregano

1/2 teaspoon salt (optional)

1/2 teaspoon cumin seeds

3 green onions, thinly sliced

1/3 to 1/2 cup chopped fresh cilantro

Combine broth, rice, chiles, yellow onion, oregano, salt, if desired, and cumin in large saucepan. Bring to a boil, uncovered, over high heat. Reduce heat to low; cover and simmer 18 minutes or until liquid is absorbed and rice is tender. Stir in green onions and cilantro.

Makes 6 servings

Nutrients per Serving: 3/4 cup

Calories 134	**Fiber** 1g
Fat 1g (sat 0g)	**Cholesterol** 1mg
Protein 3g	**Sodium** 99mg
Carbohydrate 27g	

Exchanges: 1-1/2 starch, 1/2 vegetable

Green Chili Rice

Broccoli & Cauliflower Stir-Fry

Quick Recipe   *(Pictured at right)*

> **2 sun-dried tomatoes** (not packed in oil)
> **1 tablespoon plus 1 teaspoon** reduced-sodium soy sauce
> **1 tablespoon rice wine vinegar**
> **1 teaspoon brown sugar**
> **1 teaspoon dark sesame oil**
> **1/8 teaspoon red pepper flakes**
> **2-1/4 teaspoons canola oil**
> **1 clove garlic,** finely chopped
> **2 cups fresh cauliflower florets**
> **2 cups fresh broccoli florets**
> **1/3 cup thinly sliced red or green bell pepper**

1. Place tomatoes in small bowl; cover with boiling water. Let stand 5 minutes; drain. Coarsely chop.

2. Meanwhile, blend soy sauce, vinegar, brown sugar, sesame oil and red pepper flakes in small bowl; set aside.

3. Heat oil in wok or large nonstick skillet over medium-high heat until hot. Add garlic; stir-fry 30 seconds. Add cauliflower and broccoli; stir-fry 4 minutes. Add tomatoes and bell pepper; stir-fry 1 minute or until vegetables are crisp-tender. Add reserved soy sauce mixture; cook and stir until heated through. Serve immediately.   *Makes 2 servings*

Nutrients per Serving: 1/2 of total recipe

Calories 155	**Fiber** 6g
Fat 8g (sat 1g)	**Cholesterol** 0mg
Protein 6g	**Sodium** 467mg
Carbohydrate 19g	

Exchanges: 3-1/2 vegetable, 1-1/2 fat

Smoked Turkey, Ripe Olive and Lentil Salad

Quick Recipe

> **3 tablespoons olive oil**
> **3 tablespoons orange juice**
> **2-1/2 tablespoons sherry vinegar** or apple cider vinegar
> **1 shallot,** thinly sliced into strips, about 1-1/2 tablespoons
> **2 teaspoons chopped orange zest**
> **1/4 teaspoon salt**
> **1/8 teaspoon black pepper**
> **3 cups cooked lentils**
> **1-1/4 cups diced peeled cooked beets**
> **1/2 cup orange segments,** halved
> **3/4 pound diced smoked turkey**
> **1 cup California Ripe Olives,** halved
> **3 ounces watercress**

1. In a large mixing bowl, whisk together olive oil, orange juice, sherry vinegar, shallot, orange zest, salt and pepper. Divide into 2 large mixing bowls and set aside.

2. Toss lentils, beets and orange segments with 1 bowl of the vinaigrette. Mix smoked turkey, California Ripe Olives and watercress in the remaining bowl. To serve, divide lentil mixture among serving plates. Top each serving with 1/2 cup smoked turkey mixture.

Makes 6 servings

Favorite recipe from **California Olive Industry**

Nutrients per Serving: about 2 cups salad

Calories 298	**Fiber** 10g
Fat 12g (sat 2g)	**Cholesterol** 36mg
Protein 20g	**Sodium** 843mg
Carbohydrate 30g	

Exchanges: 2 starch, 2 lean meat, 1 fat

Greens and Broccoli Salad with Peppy Vinaigrette

Quick Recipe

4 sun-dried tomato halves (not packed in oil)
    Boiling water
3 cups torn red leaf or green leaf lettuce
1-1/2 cups fresh broccoli florets
1 cup sliced fresh mushrooms
1/3 cup sliced radishes
2 tablespoons water
1 tablespoon balsamic vinegar
1 teaspoon canola oil
1/4 teaspoon chicken bouillon granules
1/4 teaspoon dried chervil
1/4 teaspoon dry mustard
1/8 teaspoon ground red pepper (cayenne)

1. Place tomatoes in small bowl; cover with boiling water. Let stand 5 minutes; drain. Chop tomatoes. Combine tomatoes, lettuce, broccoli, mushrooms and radishes in large salad bowl.

2. Combine 2 tablespoons water, vinegar, oil, bouillon granules, chervil, mustard and ground red pepper in jar with tight-fitting lid. Cover; shake well. Add to salad; toss to combine.

Makes 4 servings

Nutrients per Serving: 1-1/4 cups salad with vinaigrette

Calories 54	**Fiber** 2g
Fat 2g (sat <1g)	**Cholesterol** 0mg
Protein 3g	**Sodium** 79mg
Carbohydrate 9g	

Exchanges: 2 vegetable

Salad Primavera

Quick Recipe

6 cups torn romaine lettuce
1 package (9 ounces) frozen artichoke hearts, thawed, drained and cut into bite-size pieces
1 cup chopped watercress
1 medium orange, peeled and segments halved
1/2 cup chopped red bell pepper
1/4 cup chopped green onions
    Citrus-Caper Dressing (recipe follows)
2 tablespoons freshly grated Parmesan cheese

Combine lettuce, artichoke hearts, watercress, orange segments, bell pepper and green onions in large bowl. Prepare Citrus-Caper Dressing; toss with lettuce mixture. Sprinkle with Parmesan before serving. *Makes 8 servings*

Citrus-Caper Dressing

1/3 cup orange juice
1/4 cup white wine vinegar
2 tablespoons chopped fresh parsley
1 tablespoon minced capers
2 teaspoons Dijon mustard
1 teaspoon sugar
1 teaspoon minced garlic
1/4 teaspoon black pepper
1/4 teaspoon olive oil

Combine all ingredients in jar or bottle with tight-fitting lid; shake well. Refrigerate until ready to serve. Shake well before serving.

Makes about 1/2 cup

Nutrients per Serving: 1 cup salad (with 1 tablespoon dressing and 3/4 teaspoon grated Parmesan)

Calories 55	**Fiber** 3g
Fat 1g (sat <1g)	**Cholesterol** 1mg
Protein 3g	**Sodium** 102mg
Carbohydrate 10g	

Exchanges: 2 vegetable

Zucchini Delight

(Pictured below)

1 can (about 10 ounces) condensed reduced-fat reduced-sodium tomato soup, undiluted

1 tablespoon lemon juice

1 teaspoon sugar

2 cloves garlic, minced

1/2 teaspoon salt

6 cups 1/2-inch zucchini slices (about 1-1/2 pounds)

1 cup *each* thinly sliced onion, coarsely chopped green bell pepper and sliced fresh mushrooms

2 tablespoons grated Parmesan cheese

1. Combine soup, lemon juice, sugar, garlic and salt in large saucepan. Add zucchini, onion, bell pepper and mushrooms; mix well. Bring to a boil.

2. Reduce heat. Cover and cook 20 to 25 minutes or until vegetables are crisp-tender, stirring occasionally. Sprinkle with cheese before serving.   *Makes 6 servings*

Nutrients per Serving: 1 cup

Calories 92	**Fiber** 3g
Fat 2g (sat <1g)	**Cholesterol** 1mg
Protein 4g	**Sodium** 426mg
Carbohydrate 18g	

Exchanges: 3-1/2 vegetable

Zucchini Delight

Maple-Glazed Carrots & Shallots

Maple-Glazed Carrots & Shallots

 low fat · meatless

Quick Recipe   *(Pictured above)*

    1 package (16 ounces) baby carrots
    1 tablespoon butter
1/2 cup thinly sliced shallots
    2 tablespoons reduced-fat maple-flavored
        pancake syrup
1/4 teaspoon salt
1/8 teaspoon white pepper

1. Place carrots in medium saucepan; add enough water to cover. Bring to a boil over high heat. Reduce heat; simmer 8 to 10 minutes or until carrots are tender. Drain; set carrots aside.

2. In same saucepan, melt butter over medium-high heat. Add shallots; cook and stir 3 to 4 minutes or until shallots are tender and begin to brown. Add carrots, syrup, salt and pepper; cook and stir 1 to 2 minutes or until carrots are coated and heated through.

Makes 4 servings

Nutrients per Serving: about 3/4 cup

Calories 82	**Fiber** 3g
Fat 3g (sat 2g)	**Cholesterol** 8mg
Protein <1g	**Sodium** 284mg
Carbohydrate 14g	

Exchanges: 2-1/2 vegetable, 1/2 fat

ൟ ൟ ൟ

Finger-Lickin' Chicken Salad

 cooking for 1 or 2

Quick Recipe

1/2 cup cubed roasted boneless skinless
        chicken breast
1/2 stalk celery, cut into 1-inch pieces
1/4 cup drained mandarin orange segments
1/4 cup red seedless grapes
    2 tablespoons lemon sugar-free fat-free
        yogurt
    1 tablespoon reduced-fat mayonnaise
1/4 teaspoon reduced-sodium soy sauce
1/8 teaspoon pumpkin pie spice or ground
        cinnamon

1. Toss together chicken, celery, oranges and grapes in small bowl. Combine yogurt, mayonnaise, soy sauce and pumpkin pie spice in another small bowl.

2. To serve, dip chicken mixture into dipping sauce.   *Makes 1 serving*

Serving Suggestion: Thread the chicken onto wooden skewers alternately with celery, orange segments and grapes.

Nutrients per Serving: 1 salad

Calories 207	**Fiber** 1g
Fat 6g (sat 1g)	**Cholesterol** 64mg
Protein 24g	**Sodium** 212mg
Carbohydrate 15g	

Exchanges: 1 fruit, 3-1/2 lean meat

Polenta Triangles

(Pictured on page 104)

1/2 cup uncooked yellow corn grits
1-1/2 cups reduced-sodium chicken broth, divided
2 cloves garlic, minced
1/2 cup crumbled feta cheese
1 medium red bell pepper, roasted,* peeled and finely chopped

*Place bell pepper on foil-lined broiler pan; broil 15 minutes or until blackened on all sides, turning every 5 minutes. Remove pepper to paper bag. Close bag; let stand 15 minutes before peeling.

1. Combine grits and 1/2 cup chicken broth in small bowl; set aside. Pour remaining 1 cup broth into large heavy saucepan; bring to a boil. Add garlic and moistened grits; mix well. Return to a boil. Reduce heat to low. Cover; cook 20 minutes. Remove from heat; add feta cheese. Stir until cheese is completely melted. Add roasted bell pepper; mix well.

2. Spray 8-inch square pan with nonstick cooking spray. Spoon grits mixture into prepared pan. With wet fingertips, press grits evenly into pan. Refrigerate until cold.

3. Spray grid with cooking spray. Prepare grill for direct grilling. Turn polenta out onto cutting board; cut into 4 (2-inch) squares. Cut each square diagonally into 2 triangles.

4. Place polenta triangles on grid. Grill over medium-high heat 1 minute or until bottoms are lightly browned. Turn triangles over; grill until browned and crisp. Serve warm or at room temperature. *Makes 8 servings*

Nutrients per Serving: 1 triangle

Calories 62	**Fiber** <1g
Fat 2g (sat 1g)	**Cholesterol** 6mg
Protein 3g	**Sodium** 142mg
Carbohydrate 9g	

Exchanges: 1 starch

Zucchini-Tomato Bake

1 pound eggplant, coarsely chopped (about 4 cups)
2 cups zucchini slices
2 cups sliced fresh mushrooms
3 sheets (18×12 inches each) heavy-duty foil, lightly sprayed with nonstick cooking spray
2 teaspoons olive oil
1/2 cup chopped onion
1/2 cup chopped fennel bulb (optional)
2 cloves garlic, minced
1 can (about 14 ounces) whole tomatoes, undrained
1 tablespoon tomato paste
2 teaspoons dried basil
1 teaspoon sugar

1. Preheat oven to 400°F. Divide eggplant, zucchini and mushrooms into 3 portions. Arrange each portion on foil sheet.

2. Heat oil in small skillet over medium heat. Add onion, fennel, if desired, and garlic; cook and stir 3 to 4 minutes or until onion is tender. Add tomatoes with juice, tomato paste, basil and sugar. Cook and stir about 4 minutes or until sauce thickens.

3. Pour sauce over eggplant mixture. Double-fold sides and ends of foil to seal packets, leaving head space for heat circulation. Place on baking sheet.

4. Bake 40 minutes. Remove from oven. Carefully open 1 end of each packet to allow steam to escape. Transfer vegetables and sauce to serving dish. *Makes 6 servings*

Nutrients per Serving: 3/4 cup

Calories 71	**Fiber** 3g
Fat 2g (sat 0g)	**Cholesterol** 0mg
Protein 3g	**Sodium** 109mg
Carbohydrate 13g	

Exchanges: 2 vegetable, 1/2 fat

Pork Salad Toss with Balsamic Glaze

(Pictured at right)

1/2 cup balsamic vinegar

2 cups fresh cauliflower florets

1 cup fresh snow peas

1 cup vegetable broth

1 medium red bell pepper, cored, seeded and thinly sliced

1/4 pound (about 1/2 cup) thinly sliced cooked lean pork tenderloin

4 cups mixed salad greens

2 tablespoons honey-roasted sunflower seeds

Freshly ground black pepper (optional)

1. Boil vinegar in small saucepan over medium-high heat about 8 minutes or until liquid is reduced by two thirds and becomes syrupy.* Set aside.

2. Combine cauliflower, snow peas, broth, bell pepper and pork in medium skillet. Cook, covered, over medium-high heat 15 minutes or until vegetables are tender, stirring every 5 minutes.

3. Serve mixture warm over salad greens. Drizzle with reserved balsamic glaze. Sprinkle each serving with sunflower seeds. Season with freshly ground black pepper, if desired.

Makes 2 servings

Watch carefully, as reduction will occur very quickly towards end of cooking time. If overcooked, reduction could scorch.

Nutrients per Serving: 1/2 of total recipe

Calories 245	**Fiber** 7g
Fat 8g (sat 1g)	**Cholesterol** 45mg
Protein 23g	**Sodium** 609mg
Carbohydrate 25g	

Exchanges: 5 vegetable, 2-1/2 lean meat

Thai Pasta Salad with Peanut Sauce

Quick Recipe

1/4 cup evaporated fat-free milk

1 tablespoon plus 1-1/2 teaspoons creamy peanut butter

1 tablespoon plus 1-1/2 teaspoons finely chopped red onion

1 teaspoon lemon juice

3/4 teaspoon brown sugar

1/2 teaspoon reduced-sodium soy sauce

1/8 teaspoon red pepper flakes

1/2 teaspoon finely chopped fresh gingerroot

1 cup hot cooked whole wheat spaghetti

2 teaspoons finely chopped green onion

1. Combine evaporated milk, peanut butter, red onion, lemon juice, brown sugar, soy sauce and red pepper flakes in medium saucepan. Bring to a boil over high heat, stirring constantly. Boil 2 minutes, stirring constantly.

2. Reduce heat to medium-low. Add gingerroot; mix well. Add spaghetti; toss to coat.

3. Top each serving with green onion.

Makes 2 servings

Nutrients per Serving: 1/2 of total recipe

Calories 187	**Fiber** 3g
Fat 6g (sat 1g)	**Cholesterol** 38mg
Protein 9g	**Sodium** 85mg
Carbohydrate 27g	

Exchanges: 1-1/2 starch, 1/2 milk, 1 fat

Tip

Peanut butter, promoted as a health food at the 1904 World's Fair in St. Louis, has been found, in recent years, to actually help protect against heart disease when included in a heart healthy eating plan.

Pork Salad Toss with Balsamic Glaze

Carrot and Parsnip Purée

Carrot and Parsnip Purée

(Pictured above)

1 pound carrots, peeled
1 pound parsnips, peeled
1 cup chopped onion
1-1/4 cups vegetable broth, divided
1 tablespoon butter
1/8 teaspoon ground nutmeg

1. Cut carrots and parsnips widthwise into 1/2-inch pieces.

2. Combine carrots, parsnips, onion and 1 cup vegetable broth in medium saucepan; cover. Bring to a boil over high heat. Reduce heat; simmer, covered, 20 to 22 minutes or until vegetables are very tender.

3. Drain vegetables. Combine vegetables, butter, nutmeg and remaining 1/4 cup broth in food processor container; process until smooth. Serve immediately, or transfer to microwave-safe dish and chill up to 24 hours.

4. To reheat, cover and microwave on HIGH 6 to 7 minutes, stirring after 4 minutes of cooking. *Makes 6 servings*

Nutrients per Serving: about 1/2 cup purée

Calories 130	**Fiber** 4g
Fat 2g (sat 1g)	**Cholesterol** 6mg
Protein 2g	**Sodium** 96mg
Carbohydrate 27g	

Exchanges: 1 starch, 2 vegetable, 1/2 fat

Crab Cobb Salad

Quick Recipe

12 cups torn romaine lettuce
2 cans (6 ounces each) crabmeat, drained, flaked and cartilage removed
2 cups diced ripe tomatoes or halved cherry tomatoes
1/4 cup crumbled blue or Gorgonzola cheese
1/4 cup imitation bacon bits
3/4 cup fat-free Italian or Caesar salad dressing
Black pepper

1. Arrange lettuce on large serving platter. Arrange crabmeat, tomatoes, blue cheese and bacon bits over lettuce.

2. Just before serving, drizzle dressing evenly over salad. Sprinkle with pepper to taste.
Makes 8 servings

Nutrients per Serving: 1-3/4 cups salad with dressing

Calories 110	**Fiber** 2g
Fat 3g (sat 1g)	**Cholesterol** 46mg
Protein 12g	**Sodium** 666mg
Carbohydrate 8g	

Exchanges: 1-1/2 vegetable, 1-1/2 lean meat

Chicken Waldorf Salad

Quick Recipe

- **2 cups cubed or shredded cooked chicken breast**
- **2 cups chopped, cored Red Delicious apples**
- **1 cup sliced celery**
- **2/3 cup halved seedless grapes**
- **1/4 cup chopped pecans, toasted**
- **1/2 cup fat-free mayonnaise**
- **1/2 cup fat-free sour cream**
- **3 to 4 teaspoons lemon juice**
- **2 teaspoons Dijon-style mustard**
- **1/3 cup EQUAL® SPOONFUL***
- **Salt and pepper**
- **Red leaf lettuce**
- **1/4 cup chopped pecans (optional)**

*May substitute 8 packets EQUAL® sweetener.

• Combine chicken, apples, celery, grapes and 1/4 cup pecans in bowl. Blend mayonnaise, sour cream, lemon juice, mustard and Equal®; stir into chicken mixture. Season to taste with salt and pepper.

• Spoon salad onto lettuce-lined plates; sprinkle with additional 1/4 cup pecans, if desired.

Makes 4 servings

Variation: Cubed, lean smoked ham can be substituted for the chicken, and pineapple chunks can be substituted for the grapes. Spoon the salad into a hollowed-out pineapple half to serve. (Note: These changes will make a difference in the nutritional analysis.)

Nutrients per Serving: 1-1/4 cups salad (without salt and pepper seasoning)

Calories 251	**Fiber** 3g
Fat 8g (sat 1g)	**Cholesterol** 48mg
Protein 21g	**Sodium** 489mg
Carbohydrate 27g	

Exchanges: 1-1/2 fruit, 3 lean meat

Raspberry Mango Salad

meatless

Quick Recipe   *(Pictured below)*

- **2 cups arugula or baby spinach**
- **1 cup torn Bibb or Boston lettuce**
- **1 cup cubed peeled mango (1 mango)**
- **3/4 cup fresh raspberries**
- **1/2 cup watercress, stems removed**
- **1/4 cup crumbled blue cheese**
- **1 tablespoon water**
- **1 tablespoon olive oil**
- **1 tablespoon raspberry vinegar**
- **1/8 teaspoon salt**
- **1/8 teaspoon black pepper**

1. Combine arugula, lettuce, mango, raspberries, watercress and cheese in medium bowl.

2. Combine remaining ingredients in small jar with tight-fitting lid; shake. Pour over salad; toss to coat. Serve immediately.

Makes 4 servings

Nutrients per Serving: 1 cup salad with vinaigrette

Calories 98	**Fiber** 2g
Fat 8g (sat 3g)	**Cholesterol** 8mg
Protein 3g	**Sodium** 227mg
Carbohydrate 12g	

Exchanges: 1/2 fruit, 1 vegetable, 1 fat

Raspberry Mango Salad

Scalloped Potatoes

meatless

(Pictured at right)

2 tablespoons butter
3 tablespoons all-purpose flour
2-1/2 cups fat-free milk
1/4 cup grated Parmesan cheese
1/4 teaspoon black pepper
2 pounds baking potatoes, peeled and thinly sliced
1 teaspoon salt
1/8 teaspoon ground nutmeg
2/3 cup shredded reduced-fat Swiss cheese, divided
3 tablespoons thinly sliced chives, divided

1. Preheat oven to 350°F. Spray 2-quart glass casserole with nonstick cooking spray.

2. Melt butter in medium saucepan; stir in flour and cook over medium-low heat 1 to 2 minutes, stirring constantly. Using wire whisk, gradually stir in milk; bring to a boil. Cook, whisking constantly, 1 to 2 minutes or until mixture thickens. Stir in Parmesan cheese; season with pepper.

3. Layer one third of potatoes in bottom of prepared casserole. Sprinkle with dash of salt, nutmeg, one third of Swiss cheese and 1 tablespoon chives. Spoon one third of white sauce over chives. Repeat layers, ending with white sauce.

4. Bake 1 hour and 15 minutes or until potatoes are fork-tender. Cool slightly before serving.

Makes 8 servings

Nutrients per Serving: 1/3 cup potatoes

Calories 197	**Fiber** 2g
Fat 4g (sat 3g)	**Cholesterol** 14mg
Protein 9g	**Sodium** 423mg
Carbohydrate 31g	

Exchanges: 1-1/2 starch, 1/2 milk, 1/2 lean meat

Spinach and Mushroom Risotto

Quick Recipe

Olive oil cooking spray
1/2 pound mushrooms, sliced
2 teaspoons dried basil
2 teaspoons minced garlic
1/4 teaspoon black pepper
1-2/3 cups water
1-1/2 cups uncooked arborio rice
1 can (about 14 ounces) reduced-sodium chicken broth
1 can (about 10-3/4 ounces) reduced-fat reduced-sodium condensed cream of mushroom soup, undiluted
3 cups packed washed and stemmed spinach, chopped
6 tablespoons chopped walnuts, toasted*
1/4 cup grated Parmesan cheese

*To toast walnuts, spread in a single layer on baking sheet. Bake in preheated 350°F oven 8 to 10 minutes or until golden brown, stirring frequently.

1. Spray 3-quart saucepan with cooking spray; heat over high heat. Add mushrooms, basil, garlic and pepper; cook and stir 3 to 4 minutes or until mushrooms are tender.

2. Stir in water, rice, broth and soup; cook and stir until well blended and mixture begins to boil. Reduce heat to low. Cover; simmer gently 12 minutes or until rice is just tender but still firm, stirring twice during cooking.

3. Stir in spinach; cover and let stand 5 to 7 minutes or until spinach is wilted.

4. Sprinkle with walnuts and cheese before serving.

Makes 8 servings

Nutrients per Serving: 1 cup risotto

Calories 219	**Fiber** 3g
Fat 5g (sat 1g)	**Cholesterol** 2mg
Protein 8g	**Sodium** 250mg
Carbohydrate 37g	

Exchanges: 1-1/2 starch, 2-1/2 vegetable, 1 fat

Jalapeño Coleslaw

Jalapeño Coleslaw

 low fat / meatless

(Pictured above)

6 cups coleslaw mix (without dressing)
2 medium fresh tomatoes, seeded and chopped
6 green onions, coarsely chopped
2 jalapeño peppers,* finely chopped
1/4 cup cider vinegar
3 tablespoons honey
1 teaspoon salt

Jalapeño peppers can sting and irritate the skin, so wear rubber gloves when handling peppers and do not touch your eyes.

1. Combine coleslaw mix, tomatoes, green onions, jalapeño peppers, vinegar, honey and salt in serving bowl; mix well. Cover; chill at least 2 hours before serving.

2. Stir well immediately before serving.
Makes 8 servings

Hint: For a milder coleslaw, discard the jalapeños' seeds and veins—where most of the heat is stored.

Nutrients per Serving: about 1 cup coleslaw

Calories 47	**Fiber** 2g
Fat <1g (sat <1g)	**Cholesterol** 0mg
Protein 1g	**Sodium** 304mg
Carbohydrate 12g	

Exchanges: 1/2 starch, 1 vegetable

Double Mango-Shrimp Salad

cooking for 1 or 2

Quick Recipe

3 tablespoons picante sauce or salsa
1 tablespoon mango or peach chutney
1 tablespoon Dijon mustard
1 tablespoon lime juice
4 cups torn Boston or red leaf lettuce
6 ounces medium or large cooked shrimp, peeled and deveined
1/2 cup diced avocado
1/2 cup diced peeled mango or papaya
1/3 cup red or yellow bell pepper strips
2 tablespoons chopped fresh cilantro (optional)

1. Combine picante sauce, chutney, mustard and lime juice in small bowl; mix well.

2. Combine remaining ingredients in medium bowl. Add chutney mixture; toss well. Transfer to serving plates.
Makes 2 servings

Nutrients per Serving: 2-1/4 cups salad

Calories 221	**Fiber** 4g
Fat 7g (sat 1g)	**Cholesterol** 166mg
Protein 21g	**Sodium** 583mg
Carbohydrate 19g	

Exchanges: 1/2 fruit, 2-1/2 vegetable, 2-1/2 lean meat

Roasted Vegetable Salad

high fiber · **meatless** · cooking for 1 or 2

Quick Recipe   (Pictured at bottom right)

- 1 cup green or yellow bell pepper pieces
- 1 cup cherry tomatoes
- 1 cup thinly sliced carrots
- 1 cup sliced fresh mushrooms
- 1/2 cup chopped white, Vidalia or other sweet onion
- 2 tablespoons pitted and chopped kalamata olives
- 2 teaspoons lemon juice, divided
- 1 teaspoon dried oregano
- 1 teaspoon olive oil
- 1/2 teaspoon black pepper
- 1 teaspoon sugar substitute (optional)
- 3 cups washed and stemmed spinach

1. Preheat oven to 375°F. Toss together bell pepper, tomatoes, carrots, mushrooms, onion, olives, 1 teaspoon lemon juice, oregano, oil and black pepper on baking sheet.

2. Bake 20 minutes, stirring once. Remove from oven and mix in remaining 1 teaspoon lemon juice and sugar substitute, if desired. Serve vegetable mixture warm over spinach.

Makes 2 servings

Nutrients per Serving: 1/2 of total recipe

Calories 121	**Fiber** 6g
Fat 4g (sat <1g)	**Cholesterol** 0mg
Protein 5g	**Sodium** 314mg
Carbohydrate 20g	

Exchanges: 4 vegetable, 1 fat

Tip

Kalamata olives have a rich, fruity flavor and a dark purplish color. They are usually marinated in wine vinegar and packed in either vinegar or oil. Their flesh is often slit to allow the marinade to penetrate the skin.

Carolyn's Mandarin Salmon Salad

cooking for 1 or 2

Quick Recipe

- 1 skinless salmon fillet (8 ounces)
- 1/4 teaspoon *each* salt and pepper
- 4 cups spring greens salad mix
- 1 can (8 ounces) mandarin oranges, rinsed and drained
- 2 tablespoons roughly chopped walnuts
- 1 tablespoon Dijon mustard
- 1 tablespoon balsamic vinegar

1. Season fillet with salt, if desired, and black pepper. Broil, grill or pan-fry salmon about 4 minutes per side, depending on thickness of fillet, or until meat is firm to the touch and flakes when tested with fork.

2. Divide greens between 2 plates. Cut fillet in half; place half on each plate over greens. Sprinkle with orange segments and walnuts. Combine mustard and vinegar in small bowl. Drizzle over each salad.   *Makes 2 servings*

Nutrients per Serving: 2-1/2 cups salad with 1/2 of salmon fillet

Calories 331	**Fiber** 4g
Fat 16g (sat 4g)	**Cholesterol** 56mg
Protein 25g	**Sodium** 543mg
Carbohydrate 18g	

Exchanges: 1 fruit, 1 vegetable, 3 lean meat, 1 fat

Roasted Vegetable Salad

Soups & Sandwiches

✿ ✿ ✿

Stanley Sandwiches

Quick Recipe   *(Pictured at left)*

> 1/2 cup shredded carrot
> 2 tablespoons reduced-fat ranch salad dressing
> 1/2 (12-ounce) loaf focaccia bread
> 3 lettuce leaves
> 6 ounces deli-sliced lean roast beef, roast chicken breast
>   or roast turkey breast

1. Combine carrot and salad dressing in small bowl. Split focaccia in half horizontally. Place lettuce leaves on bottom half. Top with meat, then carrot mixture. Top with remaining focaccia half.

2. Cut into 3 sandwiches to serve.   *Makes 3 servings*

Nutrients per Serving: 1 sandwich

Calories 255
Fat 6g (sat 1g)
Protein 16g
Carbohydrate 33g

Fiber 1g
Cholesterol 23mg
Sodium 847mg

Exchanges: 2 starch, 1/2 vegetable, 1-1/2 lean meat, 1/2 fat

Clockwise from top left: *Stanley Sandwich, Steak and Black Bean Chili (page 144), Portobello Mushroom Burger (page 139) and Creamy Cauliflower Bisque (page 143)*

Chicken and Dumplings Stew

(Pictured at right)

2 cans (about 14 ounces each) reduced-sodium chicken broth

1 pound boneless skinless chicken breasts, cut into bite-size pieces

1 cup diagonally sliced carrots

3/4 cup diagonally sliced celery

1 medium onion, cut into small wedges

3 small new potatoes, unpeeled and cut into cubes

1/2 teaspoon dried rosemary, crushed

1/2 teaspoon black pepper

3 tablespoons all-purpose flour

1/3 cup water

1 can (about 14 ounces) diced tomatoes, drained *or* 1-1/2 cups diced seeded fresh tomatoes

Dumplings

3/4 cup all-purpose flour

1 teaspoon baking powder

1/4 teaspoon *each* salt and onion powder

1 to 2 tablespoons finely chopped fresh parsley

1/4 cup egg substitute

1/4 cup 1% milk

1 tablespoon canola oil

1. Bring broth to a boil in Dutch oven; add chicken. Cover; simmer 3 minutes. Add carrots, celery, onion, potatoes, rosemary and pepper. Cover; simmer 10 minutes.

2. Combine 3 tablespoons flour and water in small bowl. Reduce heat of Dutch oven; stir in tomatoes and dissolved flour. Bring to a boil; cook and stir until broth thickens.

3. For dumplings, combine 3/4 cup flour, baking powder, salt and onion powder in medium bowl; blend in parsley. Combine egg substitute, milk and oil in small bowl; stir into flour mixture just until dry ingredients are moistened.

4. Return broth mixture to a boil. Drop 8 tablespoonfuls of dumpling batter into broth; cover tightly. Reduce heat; simmer 18 to

20 minutes. (Do not lift lid.) Dumplings are done when toothpick inserted into centers comes out clean. *Makes 6 servings*

Nutrients per Serving: about 1-1/2 cups stew with 1-1/3 dumplings

Calories 281	**Fiber** 2g
Fat 5g (sat 1g)	**Cholesterol** 47mg
Protein 25g	**Sodium** 645mg
Carbohydrate 34g	

Exchanges: 2 starch, 1 vegetable, 2 lean meat

❧ ❧ ❧

Open-Faced Garbanzo Melts

Quick Recipe

1 can (about 15 ounces) chickpeas, rinsed and drained

1/4 cup chopped fresh parsley

1/4 cup reduced-fat cream cheese, softened

1 tablespoon chopped fresh dill *or* 1 teaspoon dried dill weed

1 tablespoon fat-free milk

1/8 teaspoon black pepper

8 very thin slices wheat bread, toasted

1/4 cup shredded part-skim mozzarella cheese

Preheat broiler. Beat beans, parsley, cream cheese, dill, milk and pepper in medium bowl with electric mixer at medium-low speed about 2 minutes or until almost smooth. Spread bean mixture onto 8 slices wheat toast. Top with mozzarella cheese. Broil on ungreased baking sheet 4 inches from heat 2 to 3 minutes or until heated through and cheese is melted.

Makes 4 servings

Nutrients per Serving: 2 open-faced melts

Calories 217	**Fiber** 8g
Fat 7g (sat 4g)	**Cholesterol** 9mg
Protein 11g	**Sodium** 654mg
Carbohydrate 31g	

Exchanges: 2 starch, 1/2 lean meat, 1 fat

Chicken and Dumplings Stew

Light New Orleans Gumbo

Cooking spray
1 cup chopped onion
1 green bell pepper, chopped
3/4 cup sliced celery
4 cloves garlic, minced
2 tablespoons all-purpose flour
1 tablespoon Cajun, blackened or Creole seasoning mix
1 package JENNIE-O TURKEY STORE® Extra Lean Boneless Turkey Breast Tenderloins
1 can (14-1/2 ounces) Cajun-style or regular stewed tomatoes, undrained
1 can (14-1/2 ounces) fat-free, reduced-sodium chicken broth
1 package (10 ounces) frozen sliced okra, thawed
1/4 teaspoon hot pepper sauce
1/4 cup non-saturated-fat bacon bits
1 teaspoon filé powder (optional)
1/4 cup chopped parsley

Coat large nonstick saucepan or deep skillet with cooking spray; heat over medium heat. Add onion, bell pepper, celery and garlic; cook 8 minutes, stirring occasionally. Meanwhile, combine flour and seasoning mix in plastic or paper bag. Cut turkey into 1-inch chunks; add to bag and toss to coat. Add turkey and any remaining flour mixture from bag to saucepan; cook 5 minutes, stirring occasionally. Add tomatoes, broth, okra and hot sauce; bring to a simmer. Simmer uncovered 12 to 15 minutes or until turkey is no longer pink in center and mixture thickens, stirring occasionally. Remove from heat; stir in bacon bits and, if desired, filé powder. Ladle into bowls; top with parsley.

Makes 6 servings

Nutrients per Serving: about 1-1/4 cups gumbo

Calories 201	**Fiber** 4g
Fat 3g (sat <1g)	**Cholesterol** 46mg
Protein 28g	**Sodium** 435mg
Carbohydrate 17g	

Exchanges: 1/2 starch, 2 vegetable, 3 lean meat

Salmon Pattie Burgers

1 can (about 14 ounces) red salmon, drained
1 egg white
2 tablespoons toasted wheat germ
1 tablespoon dried onion flakes
1 tablespoon capers, drained
1/2 teaspoon dried thyme
1/4 teaspoon black pepper
4 whole wheat buns, split
2 tablespoons Dijon mustard
4 tomato slices
4 thin red onion slices *or* 8 dill pickle slices
4 lettuce leaves

1. Place salmon in medium bowl; flake salmon, and mash bones and skin with fork. (Discard bones and skin, if you prefer.) Add egg white, wheat germ, onion flakes, capers, thyme and pepper; mix well.

2. Divide into 4 portions and shape into firm patties. Place on plate; cover with plastic wrap and refrigerate 1 hour or until firm.

3. Spray large skillet with nonstick cooking spray. Cook patties over medium heat 5 minutes per side.

4. Spread cut sides of buns lightly with mustard. Place patties on bottoms of buns; top with tomato and onion slices, lettuce leaves and tops of buns.

Makes 4 servings

Note: Red salmon is more expensive and has a firm texture and deep red color. Pink salmon is less expensive and is a light pink color.

Nutrients per Serving: 1 sandwich (with 1-1/2 teaspoons Dijon)

Calories 327	**Fiber** 5g
Fat 14g (sat 3g)	**Cholesterol** 63mg
Protein 28g	**Sodium** 894mg
Carbohydrate 28g	

Exchanges: 1-1/2 starch, 1 vegetable, 3 lean meat, 1/2 fat

Crunchy Turkey Pita Pockets

high fiber

Quick Recipe   (Pictured below)

- **1/2 cup diced cooked boneless skinless turkey breast, chicken breast or deli-sliced reduced-sodium lean roast turkey breast**
- **1/4 cup coleslaw mix (without dressing)**
- **1/4 cup dried cranberries**
- **2 tablespoons shredded carrot**
- **1 tablespoon reduced-fat or fat-free mayonnaise**
- **1-1/2 teaspoons honey-mustard**
- **1 (6-inch) whole wheat pita bread round, cut in half**

1. Combine turkey, coleslaw mix, cranberries, carrot, mayonnaise and honey-mustard in medium bowl; mix well.

2. Fill pita halves with turkey mixture.

Makes 2 servings

Nutrients per Serving: 1 pita half filled with about 1/2 cup plus 1 tablespoon turkey mixture

Calories 256	**Fiber** 4g
Fat 3g (sat 1g)	**Cholesterol** 59mg
Protein 25g	**Sodium** 288mg
Carbohydrate 34g	

Exchanges: 1 starch, 1 fruit, 1/2 vegetable, 3 lean meat

Crunchy Turkey Pita Pockets

Turkey Chili

(Pictured at right)

Nonstick cooking spray
1 pound 93% lean ground turkey
1 cup chopped onion
1 cup chopped green bell pepper
3 cloves garlic, minced
3 cans (about 14 ounces each) diced tomatoes
1/2 cup water
1 tablespoon chili powder
1 teaspoon ground cinnamon
1 teaspoon ground cumin
1/2 teaspoon paprika
1/2 teaspoon dried oregano
1/2 teaspoon black pepper
1/4 teaspoon salt
1 can (about 15 ounces) pinto beans, rinsed and drained

1. Spray large skillet with cooking spray. Cook turkey, onion, bell pepper and garlic over medium-high heat about 5 minutes or until turkey begins to brown, stirring frequently to break up turkey.

2. Stir in tomatoes; cook 5 minutes. Add water, chili powder, cinnamon, cumin, paprika, oregano, black pepper and salt; mix well. Stir in beans.

3. Bring to a boil; reduce heat to medium-low. Simmer about 30 minutes or until chili thickens.
Makes 4 servings

Nutrients per Serving: 2 cups chili

Calories 333	**Fiber** 13g
Fat 8g (sat 2g)	**Cholesterol** 65mg
Protein 31g	**Sodium** 986mg
Carbohydrate 39g	

Exchanges: 1 starch, 4 vegetable, 3 lean meat

Rice and Roast Beef Sandwiches

Quick Recipe

1 small red onion, sliced into thin rings
1 teaspoon olive oil
3 cups cooked brown rice
1/2 cup whole kernel corn
1/2 cup sliced ripe olives (optional)
1/2 cup barbecue sauce
2 tablespoons lime juice
1/2 teaspoon garlic salt
1/2 teaspoon ground cumin
4 (6-inch) whole wheat pita rounds, halved and warmed
8 lettuce leaves
1 cup sliced, cooked lean roast beef
1 large tomato, seeded and chopped

Cook onion in oil in large skillet over medium-high heat until tender. Add rice, corn, olives, barbecue sauce, lime juice, garlic salt and cumin; toss until heated. Line each pita half with lettuce leaf, 1/2 cup hot rice mixture and roast beef; top with tomato.
Makes 8 (1/2 pita) sandwiches

Favorite recipe from **USA Rice**

Nutrients per Serving: 1 filled pita half

Calories 361	**Fiber** 5g
Fat 8g (sat 2g)	**Cholesterol** 69mg
Protein 30g	**Sodium** 418mg
Carbohydrate 41g	

Exchanges: 2-1/2 starch, 1/2 vegetable, 3 lean meat

Tip

Cumin is the dried fruit of a plant in the parsley family and is most popular in Asian, Middle Eastern and Mediterranean cuisine. It is available in seed and ground forms and should be stored in a cool, dark place for no more than six months.

Turkey Chili

Country Sausage and Bean Soup

Country Sausage and Bean Soup

(Pictured above)

2 cans (about 14 ounces each) reduced-sodium chicken broth
1-1/2 cups hot water
1 cup dried black beans, rinsed and sorted
1 cup chopped onion
2 bay leaves
1 teaspoon sugar substitute
1/8 teaspoon ground red pepper (cayenne)
Nonstick cooking spray
6 ounces reduced-fat country pork sausage
1 cup chopped seeded fresh tomato
1 tablespoon chili powder
1 tablespoon Worcestershire sauce
2 teaspoons olive oil
1-1/2 teaspoons ground cumin
1/2 teaspoon salt
1/4 cup chopped fresh cilantro

Slow Cooker Directions
1. Combine broth, water, beans, onion, bay leaves, sugar substitute and ground red pepper

in 3-1/2- to 4-quart slow cooker. Cover; cook on LOW 8 hours or on HIGH 4 hours. Remove bay leaves; discard.

2. Coat 10-inch nonstick skillet with cooking spray. Heat over medium-high heat until hot. Add sausage; cook until beginning to brown, stirring to break up large pieces. Drain fat.

3. Add sausage to bean mixture in slow cooker, along with remaining ingredients except cilantro. Cover; cook on HIGH 15 minutes. Top with cilantro before serving.

Makes 9 servings

Nutrients per Serving: 3/4 cup soup

Calories 159	**Fiber** 4g
Fat 6g (sat 1g)	**Cholesterol** 23mg
Protein 11g	**Sodium** 360mg
Carbohydrate 17g	

Exchanges: 1 starch, 1 lean meat, 1 fat

❧ ❧ ❧

Grilled Portobello Open-Faced Sandwich

Quick Recipe

1 portobello mushroom cap
2 teaspoons balsamic vinegar
1 tablespoon pesto sauce
1 slice bread, toasted
1 teaspoon grated Parmesan cheese

1. Preheat broiler. Sprinkle mushroom cap with balsamic vinegar. Broil 4 inches from heat 3 to 4 minutes per side or until tender.

2. Spread pesto onto toast. Top with mushroom cap. Sprinkle with Parmesan cheese. Serve immediately. *Makes 1 serving*

Nutrients per Serving: 1 open-faced sandwich

Calories 155	**Fiber** 1g
Fat 8g (sat 1g)	**Cholesterol** 2mg
Protein 4g	**Sodium** 300mg
Carbohydrate 17g	

Exchanges: 1 starch, 1 vegetable, 1-1/2 fat

Shortcut Calzones

(Pictured at bottom right)

- 2/3 cup cherry tomatoes, halved and seeded
- 1/2 cup finely chopped cooked extra-lean ground sirloin
- 1/3 cup thawed frozen chopped spinach, squeezed dry
- 1/4 cup chopped onion
- 1 tablespoon minced green olives
- 1/2 teaspoon minced garlic
- 4 ready-to-use frozen dinner rolls dough, thawed (about 1.3 ounces per roll)
- 3 teaspoons tomato paste
- 6 teaspoons shredded reduced-fat mozzarella cheese, divided
- 1/2 cup reduced-fat low-sodium marinara sauce

1. Preheat oven to 425°F. Spray baking sheet with nonstick cooking spray; set aside.

2. Mix together tomatoes, beef, spinach, onion, olives and garlic in medium bowl; set aside.

3. Roll out each dinner roll dough ball on floured surface until thin. Lay 2 dough pieces on prepared baking sheet. Spread each piece on baking sheet with 1-1/2 teaspoons tomato paste. Top each with sirloin mixture and 1-1/2 teaspoons cheese. Top with remaining 2 dough pieces. Pinch dough edges together to seal filling.

4. Bake 15 minutes or until golden and heated through. Garnish each calzone with 1 tablespoon marinara and remaining 1-1/2 teaspoons cheese. Cut each calzone in half and serve immediately. Use remaining marinara for dipping.
Makes 2 servings

Nutrients per Serving: 1 calzone (2 halves)

Calories 351	**Fiber** 7g
Fat 9g (sat 2g)	**Cholesterol** 20mg
Protein 17g	**Sodium** 912mg
Carbohydrate 51g	

Exchanges: 3 starch, 1 vegetable, 1 lean meat, 1 fat

Philly Sandwich

Quick Recipe

- 2 teaspoons canola oil
- 1 medium onion, thinly sliced
- 1 medium green bell pepper, cored, seeded and cut into strips
- 1 clove garlic, minced
- 1 boneless beef top sirloin steak (about 1 pound), trimmed of fat and cut into 4 pieces *or* 4 beef cubed steaks (about 1/4 pound each)
- 1/4 teaspoon salt
- 1/4 teaspoon black pepper
- 4 small French rolls, toasted

1. Heat oil in large skillet over medium heat. Add onion, bell pepper and garlic; cook and stir about 10 minutes or until vegetables are tender. Remove from skillet.

2. Add steak to skillet; cook over medium heat 5 minutes per side for medium or until desired doneness is reached. Season with salt and pepper. Place steaks in rolls; top with onion-pepper mixture.
Makes 4 servings

Nutrients per Serving: 1 sandwich

Calories 409	**Fiber** 2g
Fat 12g (sat 4g)	**Cholesterol** 101mg
Protein 40g	**Sodium** 521mg
Carbohydrate 34g	

Exchanges: 2 starch, 1 vegetable, 4 lean meat, 1/2 fat

Shortcut Calzone

Mediterranean Soup with Mozzarella

Nonstick cooking spray

2 medium green bell peppers, cored, seeded and chopped

1 cup chopped onion

2 cups chopped eggplant (about 8 ounces)

1 cup sliced mushrooms (about 4 ounces)

2 cloves garlic, minced

2 tablespoons dried basil, divided

3 cups water

1 can (about 14 ounces) diced tomatoes with Italian herbs

1/2 cup water or red wine

1 can (about 15 ounces) white beans, rinsed and drained

2 teaspoons sugar

1/4 teaspoon salt

1/4 cup minced fresh parsley

1-1/2 cups shredded reduced-fat mozzarella cheese

1. Spray Dutch oven with cooking spray. Heat over medium-high heat until hot. Add bell peppers and onion; cook, stirring frequently, 4 minutes or until onion is translucent.

2. Add eggplant, mushrooms, garlic and all but 1 teaspoon basil. Cook 4 minutes, stirring frequently. Add water, tomatoes and wine; stir to blend. Reduce heat; cover tightly and simmer 30 minutes, stirring occasionally.

3. Remove Dutch oven from heat. Stir in beans, sugar and salt. Cover and let stand 5 minutes. Toss remaining 1 teaspoon basil with parsley and cheese; top each serving with 1/4 cup cheese mixture. *Makes 6 servings*

Nutrients per Serving: 1-1/4 cups soup with 1/4 cup cheese topping

Calories 204	**Fiber** 6g
Fat 5g (sat 2g)	**Cholesterol** 10mg
Protein 13g	**Sodium** 714mg
Carbohydrate 27g	

Exchanges: 1 starch, 2-1/2 vegetable, 1-1/2 lean meat

Winter Squash Soup

Quick Recipe

1 tablespoon reduced-fat butter

1 tablespoon minced shallot or onions

2 cloves garlic, minced

3 sprigs fresh thyme

1 pinch dried rosemary

2 packages (10 ounces each) frozen winter (butternut) squash, thawed

1 cup reduced-sodium chicken broth

3 tablespoons fat-free milk

Fat-free sour cream (optional)

1. Melt butter in medium saucepan over medium heat. Add shallot, garlic, thyme and rosemary. Cook and stir 2 to 3 minutes or until shallot is tender.

2. Add squash and chicken broth; bring to a boil. Add milk; stir until blended.

3. Remove thyme sprigs from soup. Transfer soup to blender or food processor container; blend until smooth. (Add additional liquid to make soup thinner, if desired.) Top individual servings with sour cream, if desired. *Makes 4 servings*

Nutrients per Serving: 1 cup soup (without additional liquid)

Calories 116	**Fiber** 2g
Fat 2g (sat <1g)	**Cholesterol** <1mg
Protein 5g	**Sodium** 135mg
Carbohydrate 22g	

Exchanges: 4 vegetable, 1/2 fat

Tip

To limit the sodium in your recipes even more, try boiling the carcus of a whole chicken, cooling the broth down, then skimming the fat off the top. It's handy to freeze the broth in 1- or 2-cup portions and thaw it as needed.

Mediterranean Soup with Mozzarella

Sweet Potato Stew

Sweet Potato Stew

(Pictured above)

1 cup *each* chopped onion and celery
1 cup grated peeled sweet potato
1 cup water
**2 slices bacon, crisp-cooked and
     crumbled**
1 cup fat-free half-and-half
     Black pepper
1/4 cup minced fresh parsley

Slow Cooker Directions

1. Place vegetables, water and bacon in 3-quart slow cooker. Cover; cook on LOW 6 hours.

2. Increase heat to HIGH. Add half-and-half, using just enough to bring stew to desired consistency. Add water, if needed. Cook 30 minutes on HIGH or until hot. Season to taste with pepper. Stir in parsley.

Makes 4 servings

Nutrients per Serving: 1-1/2 cups stew

Calories 108	**Fiber** 2g
Fat 2g (sat <1g)	**Cholesterol** 13mg
Protein 5g	**Sodium** 183mg
Carbohydrate 17g	

Exchanges: 1 starch, 1/2 fat

Refreshing Gazpacho

2 cups reduced-sodium tomato juice
**1 can (about 14 ounces) reduced-sodium
     beef broth**
**1 can (about 10 ounces) condensed
     reduced-sodium tomato soup,
     undiluted**
1-1/2 cups diced peeled cucumbers
1-1/2 cups diced green bell peppers
1 cup shredded carrots
1 cup diced celery
1/2 cup sliced green onions
1/3 cup chopped fresh parsley
2 cloves garlic, minced
1 tablespoon lime juice
**2 teaspoons reduced-sodium
     Worcestershire sauce**
1/2 teaspoon salt (optional)
1/2 teaspoon dried oregano
     Fat-free sour cream (optional)
     Chopped fresh cilantro (optional)

1. Combine tomato juice, beef broth, soup, cucumbers, peppers, carrots, celery, green onions, parsley, garlic, lime juice, Worcestershire sauce, salt, if desired, and oregano in large bowl.

2. Chill at least 2 hours to allow flavors to blend.

3. Top with sour cream and cilantro, if desired.

Makes 4 servings

Nutrients per Serving: about 1-3/4 cups gazpacho

Calories 99	**Fiber** 4g
Fat 1g (sat <1g)	**Cholesterol** 0mg
Protein 4g	**Sodium** 551mg
Carbohydrate 20g	

Exchanges: 4 vegetable

Portobello Mushroom Burgers

meatless

Quick Recipe *(Pictured on page 126)*

1-1/4 teaspoons olive oil, divided
3/4 cup thinly sliced shallots
4 large portobello mushrooms, washed, patted dry and stemmed
1/8 teaspoon salt (optional)
1/8 teaspoon black pepper (optional)
2 cloves garlic, minced
1/4 cup reduced-fat mayonnaise
2 tablespoons chopped fresh basil
4 whole-grain hamburger buns
4 ounces fresh mozzarella, cut into 4 (1/4-inch-thick) slices
2 jarred roasted red bell peppers, rinsed, patted dry and cut into strips

1. Heat 1/4 teaspoon oil in medium saucepan over medium heat. Add shallots; cook 6 to 8 minutes, stirring occasionally, until golden brown and soft. Set aside.

2. Preheat broiler.

3. Drizzle 1/4 teaspoon oil over both sides of each mushroom; sprinkle both sides with salt and pepper, if desired. Place mushrooms, gill side up, on foil-lined baking sheet. Sprinkle garlic evenly among mushrooms. Broil mushrooms 4 minutes per side. Remove from oven.

4. Meanwhile, combine mayonnaise and basil in small bowl until well mixed.

5. Spread both sides of each bun with basil-mayonnaise. Divide mozzarella slices and cooked shallots evenly among buns; top each with mushroom and bell pepper strips.

Makes 4 servings

Nutrients per Serving: 1 sandwich (with 1 tablespoon basil-mayonnaise)

Calories 243	**Fiber** 3g
Fat 8g (sat 4g)	**Cholesterol** 18mg
Protein 13g	**Sodium** 511mg
Carbohydrate 30g	

Exchanges: 1-1/2 starch, 1-1/2 vegetable, 1 lean meat, 1 fat

Sweet Potato Spread Sandwich

low fat *low sodium* *meatless*

Quick Recipe *(Pictured below)*

1 medium sweet potato (about 4 ounces), peeled and chopped
2 tablespoons chopped walnuts
2 tablespoons dried cranberries
2 teaspoons sugar substitute
1/2 teaspoon ground cinnamon
4 slices reduced-calorie multi-grain bread
4 tablespoons fat-free whipped topping

1. Place sweet potato in small microwave-safe dish. Sprinkle with 2 tablespoons water. Microwave on HIGH 6 minutes. Let cool. Mash with cooking liquid.

2. Combine walnuts, dried cranberries, sugar substitute and cinnamon in small bowl; mash into potato.

3. Toast bread. Divide sweet potato mixture between 2 slices toast. Spread whipped topping over sweet potato mixture. Top with remaining toast. Cut sandwiches diagonally into halves.

Makes 4 servings

Nutrients per Serving: 1/2 sandwich

Calories 121	**Fiber** 4g
Fat 3g (sat <1g)	**Cholesterol** 2mg
Protein 3g	**Sodium** 130mg
Carbohydrate 23g	

Exchanges: 1 starch, 1/2 fruit, 1/2 fat

Sweet Potato Spread Sandwich

Tomato and Turkey Soup with Pesto

Quick Recipe   (Pictured at right)

- **1 cup uncooked rotini pasta**
- **1 can (about 10-3/4 ounces) condensed reduced-sodium tomato soup, undiluted**
- **1 cup fat-free milk**
- **2 cups (8 ounces) frozen Italian-style vegetables**
- **2 tablespoons pesto**
- **1 cup coarsely chopped cooked boneless skinless turkey breast**
- **2 tablespoons freshly grated Parmesan cheese**

1. Cook pasta according to package directions, omitting salt; drain. Set aside.

2. Meanwhile, combine soup, milk, vegetables and pesto in medium saucepan. Bring to a boil over medium heat. Reduce heat to low. Simmer, partially covered, 10 minutes or until vegetables are tender.

3. Add pasta and turkey. Cook 3 minutes or until heated through. Sprinkle with cheese just before serving.   *Makes 4 servings*

Nutrients per Serving: 1-1/2 cups soup with 1-1/2 teaspoons Parmesan cheese

Calories 285	**Fiber** 3g
Fat 7g (sat 2g)	**Cholesterol** 28mg
Protein 18g	**Sodium** 462mg
Carbohydrate 38g	

Exchanges: 2 starch, 1-1/2 vegetable, 2 lean meat

Tip

Pesto, from the Ligurian region of Italy, is an uncooked green sauce made from fresh basil, garlic, pine nuts, Parmesan cheese and olive oil. Often served with pasta, pesto can also be added to soups, marinades and dressings. It is even sometimes used as a rub for meat.

Walnut Chicken Salad Sandwich

Quick Recipe

- **2/3 cup nonfat plain yogurt**
- **1/2 cup finely chopped celery**
- **1/2 cup finely chopped fresh spinach *or* 3 tablespoons drained thawed frozen chopped spinach**
- **1/4 cup chopped green onions**
- **1 tablespoon lemon juice**
- **1 teaspoon ground mustard**
- **1 tablespoon chopped fresh dill or tarragon *or* 1/2 teaspoon dried dill weed or tarragon leaves**
- **3 cups diced cooked chicken breasts**
- **1 apple, cored and diced**
- **1/2 cup (2 ounces) chopped California walnuts**
- **Salt and black pepper (optional)**
- **4 pita breads, halved**
- **8 iceberg lettuce leaves or other crisp lettuce leaves**

In large bowl, combine yogurt, celery, spinach, onions, lemon juice, mustard and dill. Stir in chicken, apple and walnuts. Season with salt and pepper, if desired. Spoon 1/2 cup salad into each pita bread half; tuck in lettuce leaf.

Makes 8 sandwiches

Favorite recipe from **Walnut Marketing Board**

Nutrients per Serving: 1 filled pita half

Calories 245	**Fiber** 4g
Fat 8g (sat 1g)	**Cholesterol** 45mg
Protein 22g	**Sodium** 229mg
Carbohydrate 24g	

Exchanges: 1-1/2 starch, 1/2 vegetable, 2-1/2 lean meat

Tomato and Turkey Soup with Pesto

Southwest Corn and Turkey Soup

2 dried ancho chiles (each about 4 inches long) *or* 6 dried New Mexico chiles (each about 6 inches long)*

2 small zucchini (about 5 ounces each)

Nonstick cooking spray

1 medium onion, thinly sliced

3 cloves garlic, minced

1 teaspoon ground cumin

3 cans (about 14 ounces each) reduced-sodium chicken broth

1-1/2 cups shredded cooked dark turkey meat

1 can (about 15 ounces) chickpeas or black beans, rinsed and drained

1 package (10 ounces) frozen corn

1/4 cup cornmeal

1 teaspoon dried oregano

1/3 cup chopped fresh cilantro

Chiles can sting and irritate the skin, so wear rubber gloves when handling peppers and do not touch your eyes.

1. Cut stems from chiles; shake out seeds. Place chiles in medium bowl; cover with boiling water. Let stand 20 to 40 minutes or until chiles are soft; drain. Finely mince chiles; set aside.

2. Cut zucchini in half lengthwise; slice widthwise into 1/2-inch pieces. Set aside.

3. Spray large saucepan with cooking spray; heat over medium heat. Add onion; cook, covered, 3 to 4 minutes or until light golden brown, stirring several times. Add garlic and cumin; cook and stir about 30 seconds or until fragrant. Add chicken broth, zucchini, turkey, chickpeas, corn, cornmeal, oregano and reserved chiles; bring to a boil over high heat. Reduce heat to low; simmer 15 minutes or until zucchini is tender. Stir in cilantro before serving. *Makes 6 servings*

Nutrients per Serving: about 1-1/2 cups soup

Calories 243	**Fiber** 7g
Fat 5g (sat 1g)	**Cholesterol** 32mg
Protein 19g	**Sodium** 408mg
Carbohydrate 32g	

Exchanges: 2 starch, 2 lean meat

Grilled Vegetable Pitas

Quick Recipe

1 eggplant (about 1 pound), cut into 1/2-inch-thick slices

1 large portobello mushroom (5 to 6 ounces)

1 small red bell pepper, cored, seeded and quartered

1 small yellow or green bell pepper, cored, seeded and quartered

2 (1/4-inch-thick) slices large red onion

1/2 cup reduced-fat Italian or honey-Dijon salad dressing, divided

4 (8-inch) whole wheat or white pita bread rounds

1 cup shredded reduced-fat Italian cheese blend

1. Brush all sides of eggplant slices, mushroom, bell pepper quarters and onion slices with 1/3 cup dressing. Grill over medium coals, or broil 4 to 5 inches from heat 4 to 5 minutes per side or until vegetables are crisp-tender. Cut into bite-size pieces. Toss with remaining dressing.

2. Cut pita rounds in half widthwise; gently open. Fill with vegetable mixture. Top with cheese. *Makes 8 servings*

Nutrients per Serving: 1 sandwich (1 pita half filled with about 1/2 cup plus 1 tablespoon vegetable mixture and cheese)

Calories 202	**Fiber** 5g
Fat 6g (sat 2g)	**Cholesterol** 9mg
Protein 9g	**Sodium** 412mg
Carbohydrate 29g	

Exchanges: 1-1/2 starch, 1 vegetable, 1/2 lean meat, 1 fat

Creamy Cauliflower Bisque

(Pictured on page 126)

- 1 pound frozen cauliflowerets
- 1 pound baking potatoes, peeled and cut into 1-inch cubes
- 2 cans (about 14 ounces each) reduced-sodium chicken broth
- 1 cup chopped onion
- 1/2 teaspoon dried thyme
- 1/4 teaspoon garlic powder
- 1/8 teaspoon ground red pepper (cayenne)
- 1 cup evaporated fat-free milk
- 2 tablespoons butter
- 1/2 teaspoon salt
- 1/4 teaspoon coarsely ground black pepper
- 1 cup shredded reduced-fat sharp Cheddar cheese
- 1/4 cup finely chopped fresh parsley
- 1/4 cup finely sliced green onions

Slow Cooker Directions

1. Combine cauliflower, potatoes, broth, onion, thyme, garlic powder and ground red pepper in 3-1/2- to 4-quart slow cooker. Cover; cook on LOW 8 hours or on HIGH 4 hours.

2. Pour soup into blender in batches; blend until smooth, holding lid down firmly. Return puréed batches to slow cooker. Add evaporated milk, butter, salt and black pepper; stir until blended.

3. Top individual servings with cheese, parsley and green onions. *Makes 9 servings*

Nutrients per Serving: about 3/4 cup soup with 1 tablespoon plus 2 teaspoons cheese

Calories 158	**Fiber** 3g
Fat 5g (sat 2g)	**Cholesterol** 19mg
Protein 10g	**Sodium** 410mg
Carbohydrate 19g	

Exchanges: 1 starch, 1 lean meat, 1/2 fat

Sub on the Run

Quick Recipe   *(Pictured below)*

- 2 hard rolls (2 ounces each), split into halves
- 4 tomato slices
- 14 turkey pepperoni slices
- 2 ounces deli-sliced lean oven-roasted turkey breast
- 1/4 cup shredded part-skim mozzarella or reduced-fat sharp Cheddar cheese
- 1 cup coleslaw mix or shredded lettuce
- 1/4 medium green bell pepper, thinly sliced (optional)
- 2 tablespoons fat-free Italian salad dressing

Top each of two bottom halves of rolls with 2 tomato slices, 7 pepperoni slices, half of turkey, 2 tablespoons cheese, 1/2 cup coleslaw mix and half of bell pepper slices, if desired. Drizzle with salad dressing. Top with roll tops. Cut into halves, if desired. *Makes 2 servings*

Nutrients per Serving: 1 sub sandwich (2 halves)

Calories 275	**Fiber** 2g
Fat 7g (sat 2g)	**Cholesterol** 47mg
Protein 19g	**Sodium** 1,050mg
Carbohydrate 34g	

Exchanges: 1-1/2 starch, 2 vegetable, 2 lean meat

Sub on the Run

Tropical Turkey Melt

Quick Recipe

- **1 English muffin, split**
- **1 teaspoon Dijon mustard**
- **3 slices (about 1 ounce each) deli-sliced lean smoked turkey breast**
- **3 thin slices peeled papaya**
- **1 slice (1 ounce) Monterey Jack cheese**

1. Spread inside of muffin halves with mustard. Layer turkey, papaya and cheese on bottom half. Press top muffin half, mustard side down, over cheese.

2. Spray small skillet with butter-flavored cooking spray. Cook sandwich over medium heat about 4 minutes or until lightly toasted; turn and cook other side until lightly toasted and cheese is melted. Serve hot.

Makes 1 serving

Nutrients per Serving: 1 sandwich

Calories 359	**Fiber** 3g
Fat 10g (sat 6g)	**Cholesterol** 63mg
Protein 28g	**Sodium** 1,139mg
Carbohydrate 39g	

Exchanges: 1-1/2 starch, 1 fruit, 3 lean meat

Tip

The government's 2005 nutritional guidelines recommend a healthy person consume less than 2,300 mg of sodium (about 1 teaspoon of salt) per day. Deli meats, such as the turkey in this recipe, are typically very high in sodium. Some grocers do carry reduced-sodium meats. Another way to cut sodium would be to roast a whole skinless turkey breast (seasoning it very lightly, if at all) and refrigerate it for use throughout the week.

Steak and Black Bean Chili

high fiber

(Pictured on page 126)

- **1 boneless beef top sirloin steak (about 3/4 pound), trimmed of fat**
- **1 teaspoon canola oil**
- **1 cup chopped onion**
- **2 cloves garlic, minced**
- **2 cans (about 15 ounces each) black beans, rinsed and drained**
- **1 can (about 14 ounces) diced tomatoes**
- **1 cup chopped green bell pepper**
- **1 cup chopped red bell pepper**
- **1 jalapeño pepper,* minced**
- **1 cube beef bouillon**
- **2 tablespoons chili powder**
- **1/2 teaspoon sugar**
- **6 tablespoons reduced-fat sour cream**
- **1 cup chopped seeded fresh tomato**
- **2/3 cup sliced green onions**

*Jalapeño peppers can sting and irritate the skin, so wear rubber gloves when handling peppers and do not touch your eyes.

1. Cut steak into 1/2-inch cubes. Heat oil in large nonstick saucepan over medium heat until hot. Add steak, onion and garlic; cook and stir 5 minutes or until meat is no longer pink. Add beans, diced tomatoes, bell peppers, jalapeño pepper, bouillon, chili powder and sugar. Bring to a boil; reduce heat to low. Simmer, covered, 30 to 45 minutes.

2. Top individual servings with 1 tablespoon sour cream, 2 tablespoons plus 2 teaspoons chopped tomato and 2 tablespoons green onions.

Makes 6 servings

Nutrients per Serving: about 1 cup chili

Calories 277	**Fiber** 12g
Fat 7g (sat 1g)	**Cholesterol** 37mg
Protein 26g	**Sodium** 790mg
Carbohydrate 40g	

Exchanges: 2 starch, 2 vegetable, 1-1/2 lean meat

Beef Stew in Red Wine

(Pictured at right)

1-1/2 pounds boneless beef round steak, trimmed of fat, cut into 1-inch cubes
1-1/2 cups dry red wine
2 teaspoons olive oil
Grated peel of 1/2 orange
2 large cloves garlic, thinly sliced
1 bay leaf
1/2 teaspoon dried thyme
1/8 teaspoon black pepper
8 ounces fresh mushrooms, quartered
8 sun-dried tomatoes (not packed in oil), quartered
1 can (about 14 ounces) reduced-sodium beef broth
6 unpeeled small red or new potatoes, cut into wedges
1 cup peeled baby carrots
1 cup fresh pearl onions, skins removed
1 tablespoon cornstarch
2 tablespoons water

1. Combine beef, wine, oil, orange peel, garlic, bay leaf, thyme and pepper in large glass bowl. Refrigerate, covered, at least 2 hours or overnight.

2. Place beef mixture, mushrooms and tomatoes in large nonstick skillet or Dutch oven. Add enough beef broth to just cover ingredients. Bring to a boil over high heat. Cover; reduce heat to low. Simmer 1 hour. Add potatoes, carrots and onions; cover. Cook 20 to 25 minutes or until vegetables are tender and meat is no longer pink. Remove meat and vegetables from skillet; cover. Set aside. Discard orange peel and bay leaf.

3. Combine cornstarch and water in small bowl. Stir cornstarch mixture into sauce in skillet. Bring to a boil; cook and stir until sauce is slightly thickened. Return meat and vegetables to sauce; heat thoroughly.   *Makes 6 servings*

Nutrients per Serving: 1-1/3 cups stew

Calories 313	**Fiber** 3g
Fat 6g (sat 1g)	**Cholesterol** 55mg
Protein 26g	**Sodium** 304mg
Carbohydrate 31g	

Exchanges: 1-1/2 starch, 1-1/2 vegetable, 3 lean meat

Roast Beef and Feta Pitas with Cucumber Sauce

high fiber

Quick Recipe

1 medium cucumber, peeled, seeded, coarsely shredded and squeezed dry (1 cup shredded)
1/3 cup reduced-fat sour cream
1/4 cup crumbled feta cheese
2 tablespoons diced red onion
1-1/2 teaspoons lemon juice
1/4 teaspoon black pepper
4 (6-inch) whole wheat pita bread rounds, cut in half and warmed
8 washed and stemmed fresh spinach leaves
3/4 pound deli-sliced lean roast beef
8 fresh tomato slices
8 red onion slices

1. Combine cucumber, sour cream, cheese, onion, lemon juice and pepper in medium bowl. Set aside.

2. Line insides of pita pockets with spinach. Add roast beef, tomato and onion. Serve with cucumber sauce.   *Makes 4 servings*

Note: Two sandwich halves may easily fit into your personal meal plan. If eating both halves is going to put you way above your carb and nutrient limit, however, wrap up one of the halves and save it for another meal or snack.

Hint: This delicious cucumber sauce would also taste great drizzled over a sliced tomato salad or grilled or broiled fish.

Nutrients per Serving: 1 sandwich (2 filled halves) with 1/4 cup plus 2 tablespoons sauce

Calories 358	**Fiber** 7g
Fat 8g (sat 4g)	**Cholesterol** 49mg
Protein 26g	**Sodium** 1,109mg
Carbohydrate 49g	

Exchanges: 2-1/2 starch, 2 vegetable, 2 lean meat

Beef Stew in Red Wine

Black Bean Burger

Black Bean Burgers

low fat   high fiber   meatless

(Pictured above)

1 can (about 15 ounces) black beans, rinsed and drained, divided
1/3 cup green onion tops
1/4 cup plain dry bread crumbs
1/4 cup corn
1/4 cup chopped roasted red bell pepper
1 egg white
2 tablespoons chopped fresh basil
1 teaspoon onion powder
1 teaspoon dried oregano
1/2 teaspoon baking powder
1/2 teaspoon salt
1/2 teaspoon ground cumin
1/2 teaspoon black pepper, or more to taste
6 whole wheat hamburger buns
  Salsa (optional)
  Avocado slices (optional)
  Nonstick cooking spray

1. Place half of beans in bowl of food processor fitted with metal blade. Add remaining ingredients except buns, salsa, avocado and reserved beans. Pulse 30 to 40 seconds until mixture begins to hold together. Add remaining beans; pulse 3 to 4 times until just mixed. Let sit 20 minutes at room temperature for flavors to develop.

2. Preheat oven to 350°F.

3. Shape mixture into 6 patties (about 1/4 cup each). Spray 12-inch skillet with cooking spray and heat over medium heat. Add 4 patties; cook, covered, 4 to 5 minutes or until browned. Spray tops of patties with cooking spray; turn and cook 4 to 5 minutes or until browned. Repeat with remaining patties.

4. For firmer patties, place cooked patties on baking sheet; bake 12 to 15 minutes. For moister patties, serve immediately after pan-frying. Serve on buns, topped with salsa and avocado slices, if desired.

Makes 6 burgers

Hint: These patties are very tender and can break, so use 2 spatulas for support when flipping them.

Nutrients per Serving: 1 sandwich

Calories 186	**Fiber** 6g
Fat 3g (sat <1g)	**Cholesterol** 0mg
Protein 9g	**Sodium** 314mg
Carbohydrate 35g	

Exchanges: 2 starch, 1/2 lean meat

Tip

If you find you've run out of bread crumbs, try using crushed corn, wheat or rice cereal. Be sure to avoid sweetened cereals, though.

Light All-American Cheeseburgers

Quick Recipe

- **1 package JENNIE-O TURKEY STORE® Extra Lean Ground Turkey Breast**
- **1/3 cup catsup**
- **3 tablespoons seasoned dry bread crumbs**
- **2 tablespoons grated or finely chopped onion**
- **1 egg white**
- **1/2 teaspoon garlic salt (optional)**
- **1/4 teaspoon freshly ground black pepper**
- **4 slices (1/4-inch) red or yellow onion Cooking spray**
- **4 slices fat-free American cheese**
- **4 kaiser rolls, split**
- **4 slices tomato**
- **4 leaves romaine or red leaf lettuce Optional condiments: mayonnaise, catsup, mustard, sliced pickles**

In a large bowl, combine turkey, catsup, bread crumbs, onion, egg white, garlic salt and pepper. Mix well and shape into 4 patties about 1/2 inch thick. Cover and refrigerate while preparing charcoal grill. Coat patties and onion slices with cooking spray. Grill patties and onions over medium coals 6 to 7 minutes per side or until no longer pink in center. Top patties with cheese during last minute of grilling. Place rolls cut side down on grill during last 1 to 2 minutes of cooking to toast lightly. Serve patties in rolls, topped with grilled onions, tomato and lettuce. Serve with desired condiments.   *Makes 4 servings*

Nutrients per Serving: 1 sandwich

Calories 403	**Fiber** 3g
Fat 5g (sat 1g)	**Cholesterol** 59mg
Protein 45g	**Sodium** 956mg
Carbohydrate 44g	

Exchanges: 3 starch, 5 lean meat

Vegetable Beef Noodle Soup

- **Nonstick cooking spray**
- **1/2 pound beef stew meat, cut into 1/2-inch pieces**
- **3/4 cup cubed unpeeled potato (1 medium)**
- **1/2 cup sliced carrot**
- **1 tablespoon balsamic vinegar**
- **3/4 teaspoon dried thyme**
- **1/4 teaspoon black pepper**
- **2-1/2 cups reduced-sodium beef broth**
- **1 cup water**
- **1/4 cup chili sauce or ketchup**
- **2 ounces uncooked thin egg noodles**
- **3/4 cup jarred or canned pearl onions, rinsed and drained**
- **1/4 cup frozen peas**

1. Lightly spray large saucepan with cooking spray. Heat over medium-high heat until hot. Add beef; cook 3 minutes or until browned on all sides, stirring occasionally. Remove from pan.

2. Cook potato, carrot, vinegar, thyme and pepper 3 minutes in same saucepan over medium heat. Add beef broth, water and chili sauce; bring to a boil over medium-high heat. Add beef. Reduce heat to medium-low; simmer, covered, 30 minutes or until meat is nearly fork-tender.

3. Bring beef mixture to a boil over medium-high heat. Add noodles; cook, covered, 7 to 10 minutes or until noodles are tender, stirring occasionally. Add onions and peas; heat 1 minute. Serve immediately.

Makes 6 servings

Nutrients per Serving: 1-1/2 cups soup

Calories 182	**Fiber** 1g
Fat 3g (sat 1g)	**Cholesterol** 28mg
Protein 15g	**Sodium** 258mg
Carbohydrate 24g	

Exchanges: 1 starch, 1 vegetable, 1-1/2 lean meat

Desserts

≈ ≈ ≈

Cheery Cherry Brownies

Quick Recipe   *(Pictured at left)*

3/4 cup all-purpose flour
1/2 cup sugar substitute*
1/2 cup unsweetened cocoa powder
1/4 teaspoon baking soda
1/2 cup evaporated reduced-fat milk
1/3 cup butter, melted
1/4 cup egg substitute
1/4 cup honey
   1 teaspoon vanilla extract
**1/2 (15-1/2-ounce) can pitted tart red cherries (3/4 cup plus
      2 tablespoons), drained and halved**

*This recipe was tested with sucralose-based sugar substitute.

1. Preheat oven to 350°F. Grease 11×7-inch baking dish; set aside.

2. Stir together flour, sugar substitute, cocoa and baking soda in large mixing bowl. Add milk, butter, egg substitute, honey and vanilla. Stir just until blended.

3. Pour into prepared dish. Sprinkle cherries over top of chocolate mixture. Bake 13 to 15 minutes or until toothpick inserted into center comes out clean. Cool completely in dish on wire rack. Cut into 12 brownies to serve.   *Makes 12 servings*

Nutrients per Serving: 1 brownie

Calories 130	**Fiber** 2g
Fat 6g (sat 4g)	**Cholesterol** 28mg
Protein 3g	**Sodium** 110mg
Carbohydrate 18g	

Exchanges: 1 starch, 1 fat

Clockwise from top left: *Berries with Orange Scones (page 153), Grilled Banana Split (page 175), Cheery Cherry Brownie and Cheese-Filled Poached Pear (page 179)*

Bread Pudding Snacks

Bread Pudding Snacks

(Pictured above)

1-1/4 cups 2% milk

1/2 cup egg substitute

1/3 cup sugar

1 teaspoon vanilla extract

1/8 teaspoon salt

1/8 teaspoon ground nutmeg (optional)

4 cups 1/2-inch cinnamon or cinnamon-raisin bread cubes (about 6 bread slices)

1 tablespoon butter, melted

1. Preheat oven to 350°F. Line 12 medium-size muffin cups with paper liners; set aside.

2. Combine milk, egg substitute, sugar, vanilla, salt and nutmeg, if desired, in medium bowl; mix well. Add bread; mix until well moistened. Let stand at room temperature 15 minutes.

3. Spoon bread mixture evenly into prepared cups; drizzle with butter.

4. Bake 30 to 35 minutes or until snack cups are puffed and golden brown. Remove to wire rack to cool completely.   *Makes 12 servings*

Note: Snacks will puff up in the oven and fall slightly upon cooling.

Nutrients per Serving: 1 snack cup

Calories 73	**Fiber** 0g
Fat 2g (sat 2g)	**Cholesterol** 5mg
Protein 2g	**Sodium** 95mg
Carbohydrate 12g	

Exchanges: 1 starch

Berries with Orange Scones

(Pictured on page 150)

1-1/4 cups all-purpose flour
2 teaspoons sugar
1-1/2 teaspoons baking powder
1/4 teaspoon salt
1 ounce cold reduced-fat cream cheese, cut into 6 pieces
1 tablespoon cold butter, cut into 6 pieces
1 egg
1/4 cup 1% milk
1 tablespoon plus 1 teaspoon finely grated orange peel
1-1/2 cups fresh strawberries, sliced, divided
1-1/3 cups fresh blueberries, divided
2 packets sugar substitute *or* equivalent of 4 teaspoons sugar
1 tablespoon orange liqueur (optional)
1-1/2 cups no-sugar-added fat-free vanilla ice cream (optional)

1. Preheat oven to 425°F. Spray medium baking sheet with nonstick cooking spray.

2. Combine flour, sugar, baking powder and salt in medium bowl; mix well. Using pastry blender or two knives, cut cream cheese and butter into flour mixture until mixture resembles coarse crumbs. Set aside.

3. Beat egg, milk and orange peel in small bowl. Pour all at once into flour mixture; stir until just moistened. Gather dough into ball; place on lightly floured board.

4. If dough is sticky, sprinkle with a little additional flour; knead 13 times. Press dough into 8×3-inch rectangle, about 1/2 inch thick. Cut into 3 squares; cut squares diagonally in half to make 6 triangles. Place 1 inch apart on prepared baking sheet. Bake about 12 to 14 minutes or until lightly browned and set.

5. Meanwhile, purée 1/2 cup strawberries and 1/3 cup blueberries. Add remaining berries, sugar substitute and liqueur, if desired; toss to coat. Let stand 15 minutes.

6. Slice scones in half horizontally. Place 2 scone halves on each plate; top with about 1/3 cup berry sauce and 1/4 cup ice cream, if desired. Serve immediately.

Makes 6 servings

Nutrients per Serving: 2 scone halves with about 1/3 cup berry sauce

Calories 177	**Fiber** 3g
Fat 4g (sat 2g)	**Cholesterol** 43mg
Protein 5g	**Sodium** 280mg
Carbohydrate 30g	

Exchanges: 1 starch, 1 fruit, 1 fat

Mocha Cappuccino Ice Cream Pie

1/4 cup cold water
1 tablespoon instant coffee granules
4 packets sugar substitute *or* equivalent of 8 teaspoons sugar
1/2 teaspoon vanilla extract
4 cups no-sugar-added fat-free fudge marble or chocolate ice cream
1 single vanilla wafer pie crust

1. Combine water, coffee granules, sugar substitute and vanilla in small bowl; stir until granules dissolve. Set aside.

2. Combine ice cream and coffee mixture in large bowl; stir gently until liquid is blended into ice cream. Spoon into pie crust; smooth top with rubber spatula.

3. Cover with plastic wrap; freeze about 4 hours or until firm. Cut into 8 slices before serving.

Makes 8 servings

Variation: Omit pie crust and serve in dessert cups with biscotti.

Nutrients per Serving: 1 pie slice

Calories 201	**Fiber** 0g
Fat 8g (sat 2g)	**Cholesterol** 9mg
Protein 5g	**Sodium** 159mg
Carbohydrate 29g	

Exchanges: 2 starch, 1-1/2 fat

Peach Tapioca

Quick Recipe   *(Pictured at right)*

> 2 cups 2% milk
> 3 tablespoons uncooked quick-cooking tapioca
> 1 egg, lightly beaten
> 1-1/2 cups coarsely chopped peeled peaches*
> 3 tablespoons no-sugar-added apricot fruit spread
> 1 teaspoon vanilla extract

*If fresh peaches are not in season, use frozen peaches and add 2 packets sugar substitute or equivalent of 4 teaspoons sugar to milk mixture.

1. Combine milk, tapioca and egg in 1-1/2-quart saucepan; let stand 5 minutes. Stir in peaches and apricot fruit spread.

2. Cook and stir over medium heat until mixture comes to a rolling boil; cook 1 minute more. Remove from heat and stir in vanilla.

3. Cool slightly; stir. Place plastic wrap directly on surface of pudding; chill. Garnish as desired.

Makes 4 servings

Note: To quickly peel whole peaches, first plunge them into boiling water for about 1 minute.

Nutrients per Serving: about 1/2 cup pudding

Calories 155	**Fiber** 1g
Fat 4g (sat 2g)	**Cholesterol** 62mg
Protein 6g	**Sodium** 92mg
Carbohydrate 25g	

Exchanges: 1-1/2 fruit, 1/2 milk, 1/2 fat

Tip

Literally translated, phyllo means "leaf." Frozen phyllo dough can be stored for up to a year; however, once defrosted, it must be used within 3 days. Do not return the dough to the freezer, as this will cause it to become brittle.

Cherry Turnovers

Quick Recipe

> 8 frozen phyllo dough sheets, thawed
> 1/4 cup butter, melted
> 6 tablespoons no-sugar-added black cherry fruit spread
> 1-1/2 tablespoons cherry-flavored liqueur (optional)
> 1 egg
> 1 teaspoon cold water

1. Preheat oven to 400°F. Lightly brush each phyllo sheet with butter; stack. Cut through all sheets to form 6 (5-inch) squares.

2. Combine fruit spread and cherry liqueur, if desired, in small bowl. Place 1 tablespoon fruit spread mixture in center of each stack of 8 phyllo squares.

3. Brush edges of phyllo with remaining butter. Fold edges over to form triangle; gently press edges together to seal. Place on ungreased baking sheet.

4. Combine egg and water in small bowl; brush over phyllo triangles.

5. Bake 10 minutes or until golden brown. Cool on wire rack. Serve warm or at room temperature.

Makes 6 turnovers

Nutrients per Serving: 1 turnover

Calories 200	**Fiber** <1g
Fat 10g (sat 6g)	**Cholesterol** 57mg
Protein 3g	**Sodium** 215mg
Carbohydrate 23g	

Exchanges: 1-1/2 starch, 2 fat

Peach Tapioca

Mangoes and Sweet Cream

Mangoes and Sweet Cream

Quick Recipe   *(Pictured above)*

2 ounces reduced-fat cream cheese
1/2 cup vanilla reduced-fat yogurt
**1 packet sugar substitute *or* equivalent of
   2 teaspoons sugar**
1/4 teaspoon vanilla extract
**1 medium ripe mango, peeled, pitted and
   diced *or* 1 cup diced peeled peaches**

1. Combine cream cheese, yogurt, sugar substitute and vanilla in small bowl. Beat at medium speed of electric mixer until smooth. Fold in mangoes.

2. Spoon mixture into 2 dessert dishes or wine goblets.   *Makes 2 servings*

Nutrients per Serving: 2/3 cup dessert

Calories 185	**Fiber** 2g
Fat 5g (sat 4g)	**Cholesterol** 16mg
Protein 6g	**Sodium** 175mg
Carbohydrate 28g	

Exchanges: 2 fruit, 1/2 milk, 1/2 fat

Chocolate-Almond Meringue Puffs

2 tablespoons sugar
**3 packets sugar substitute *or* equivalent of
   2 tablespoons sugar**
1-1/2 teaspoons unsweetened cocoa powder
2 egg whites, at room temperature
1/2 teaspoon vanilla extract
1/4 teaspoon cream of tartar
1/4 teaspoon almond extract
1/8 teaspoon salt
1-1/2 ounces sliced almonds
**3 tablespoons sugar-free seedless
   raspberry fruit spread**

1. Preheat oven to 275°F. Combine sugar, sugar substitute and cocoa in small bowl; set aside.

2. Place egg whites in small bowl; beat at high speed of electric mixer until foamy. Add vanilla, cream of tartar, almond extract and salt; beat until soft peaks form. Add sugar mixture, 1 tablespoon at a time, beating until stiff peaks form.

3. Line baking sheet with foil. Spoon 15 equal mounds of egg white mixture onto foil. Sprinkle with almonds.

4. Bake 1 hour. Turn oven off, but do not open door. Leave puffs in oven 2 hours longer or until completely dry. Remove from oven; cool completely.

5. Stir fruit spread and spoon about 1/2 teaspoon onto each meringue just before serving.   *Makes 15 servings*

Note: These meringue puffs are best when eaten the same day they're made. If necessary, they can be stored in an airtight container. Simply add the fruit topping just prior to serving.

Nutrients per Serving: 1 meringue puff

Calories 36	**Fiber** <1g
Fat 1g (sat <1g)	**Cholesterol** 0mg
Protein 1g	**Sodium** 27mg
Carbohydrate 5g	

Exchanges: 1/2 starch

Fruit Baked Apples

1/2 cup EQUAL® SPOONFUL*
1 tablespoon cornstarch
   Pinch ground cinnamon
   Pinch ground nutmeg
2 cups apple cider or juice
1 package (6 ounces) dried mixed fruit, chopped
1 tablespoon stick butter or margarine
8 tart baking apples

*May substitute 12 packets EQUAL® sweetener.

• Combine Equal®, cornstarch, cinnamon and nutmeg in medium saucepan. Stir in cider and dried fruit. Heat to boiling.

• Reduce heat and simmer, uncovered, 10 to 15 minutes or until fruit is tender and cider mixture is reduced to about 1 cup. Stir in butter until melted.

• Remove cores from apples, cutting to, but not through, bottoms. Peel 1 inch around tops. Place apples in greased baking pan. Fill centers with fruit. Spoon remaining cider mixture over apples.

• Bake, uncovered, in preheated 350°F oven about 45 minutes or until apples are tender when pierced with a fork.   *Makes 8 servings*

Nutrients per Serving: 1 Fruit Baked Apple

Calories 164	**Fiber** 4g
Fat 2g (sat 1g)	**Cholesterol** 4mg
Protein 1g	**Sodium** 22mg
Carbohydrate 40g	

Exchanges: 2-1/2 fruit, 1/2 fat

Tip

These scrumptious, fruit-filled apples and sweet-and-creamy blueberry parfaits are just a few of the many ways you can enjoy desserts today and still feel good, knowing you're *choosing* to eat healthfully.

Ricotta Cheese and Blueberry Parfaits

Quick Recipe   (Pictured below)

1 cup ricotta cheese
1 tablespoon powdered sugar
   Grated peel of 1 lemon
1-1/2 cups fresh blueberries

1. Combine ricotta cheese, sugar and lemon peel in medium bowl; mix well.

2. Place 3 tablespoons blueberries in each of 4 parfait glasses. Add 1/4 cup ricotta cheese mixture; top with another 3 tablespoons blueberries. Garnish as desired.

Makes 4 servings

Nutrients per Serving: 2/3 cup parfait

Calories 145	**Fiber** 2g
Fat 8g (sat 5g)	**Cholesterol** 31mg
Protein 7g	**Sodium** 55mg
Carbohydrate 12g	

Exchanges: 1/2 starch, 1/2 fruit, 1 lean meat, 1 fat

Ricotta Cheese and Blueberry Parfaits

Lip-Smacking Lemon Cookies

(Pictured at right)

1/2 cup (1 stick) butter, softened
1 cup sugar
1 egg
2 tablespoons lemon juice
2 teaspoons grated lemon peel
2 cups all-purpose flour
1 teaspoon baking powder
1/8 teaspoon salt
    Dash ground nutmeg
    Yellow colored sugar (optional)

1. Beat butter in large bowl with electric mixer at medium speed until smooth. Add sugar; beat until well blended. Add egg, lemon juice and peel; beat until well blended.

2. Combine flour, baking powder, salt and nutmeg in medium bowl. Gradually add flour mixture to butter mixture at low speed, blending well after each addition.

3. Shape dough into 2 logs, each about 1-1/2 inches in diameter and 6-1/2 inches long. Roll logs in yellow sugar, if desired. Wrap each log in plastic wrap. Refrigerate 2 to 3 hours or up to 3 days.

4. Preheat oven to 350°F. Spray cookie sheets with nonstick cooking spray. Cut logs into 1/4-inch-thick slices; place 1 inch apart on prepared cookie sheets.

5. Bake about 15 minutes or until edges are lightly browned. Transfer to wire racks; cool. Store in airtight container.

Makes about 4 dozen cookies

Nutrients per Serving: 1 cookie

Calories 54	**Fiber** <1g
Fat 2g (sat 1g)	**Cholesterol** 10mg
Protein 1g	**Sodium** 32mg
Carbohydrate 8g	

Exchanges: 1/2 starch, 1/2 fat

No-Bake Coconut Cream Pie

2 tablespoons water
1 envelope plain gelatin
1 can (14-1/2 ounces) light coconut milk
1 package (8 ounces) fat-free cream cheese, cubed
9 packets sugar substitute *or* equivalent of 1/4 cup plus 2 tablespoons sugar, divided
2 teaspoons vanilla extract
1 teaspoon coconut extract
1 reduced-fat graham cracker pie crust
1/4 cup unsweetened shredded coconut

1. Place water in small microwave-safe bowl. Sprinkle gelatin over water and let stand 1 minute. Heat bowl in microwave on HIGH 20 seconds or until gelatin is completely dissolved.

2. Combine coconut milk, cream cheese, 8 packets sugar substitute, vanilla, coconut extract and gelatin mixture in blender container. Cover tightly and blend until smooth. Pour mixture into prepared crust; cover and chill about 4 hours or until firm.

3. Before serving, toast coconut in nonstick skillet over low heat until golden. When cool, toss with remaining 1 packet sugar substitute and sprinkle over pie. Cut pie into 12 slices to serve. *Makes 12 servings*

Nutrients per Serving: 1 pie slice

Calories 118	**Fiber** <1g
Fat 5g (sat 3g)	**Cholesterol** 2mg
Protein 4g	**Sodium** 175mg
Carbohydrate 13g	

Exchanges: 1 starch, 1 fat

Cocoa Nutty Bites

Quick Recipe

> **1 cup creamy unsweetened natural peanut butter**
> **1/2 cup light brown sugar, not packed**
> **1/4 cup sugar substitute***
> **1 tablespoon unsweetened cocoa powder**
> **1/2 teaspoon ground cinnamon**
> **1/4 teaspoon salt**
> **1/4 teaspoon ground ginger**
> **1 egg, beaten**

This recipe was tested with sucralose-based sugar substitute.

1. Preheat oven to 350°F.

2. Combine peanut butter, brown sugar, sugar substitute, cocoa, cinnamon, salt and ginger in medium bowl. Add egg; stir until well blended.

3. Shape dough into 24 (1-inch) balls. Place on ungreased cookie sheets. Flatten balls with fork to 1/2-inch thickness.

4. Bake 10 to 12 minutes or until cookies are firm and lightly browned. Cool on cookie sheets 5 minutes. Remove to wire racks; cool completely.   *Makes 2 dozen cookies*

Note: This simple recipe is unusual because it doesn't contain any flour—but still makes great cookies!

Nutrients per Serving: 1 cookie

Calories 85	**Fiber** 1g
Fat 5g (sat 1g)	**Cholesterol** 9mg
Protein 3g	**Sodium** 79mg
Carbohydrate 8g	

Exchanges: 1/2 starch, 1 fat

Cinnamon-Raisin Roll-Ups

Quick Recipe

> **4 ounces reduced-fat cream cheese**
> **1/2 cup shredded carrots**
> **1/4 cup golden or regular raisins**
> **1 tablespoon honey**
> **1/4 teaspoon ground cinnamon**
> **4 (7- to 8-inch) whole wheat tortillas**
> **8 thin apple wedges**

1. Combine cream cheese, carrots, raisins, honey and cinnamon in small bowl; mix well.

2. Spread tortillas evenly with cream cheese mixture, leaving 1/2-inch border around edge of each tortilla. Place 2 apple wedges down center of each tortilla; roll up. Wrap in plastic wrap. Refrigerate until ready to serve.

Makes 4 servings

Nutrients per Serving: 1 roll-up

Calories 240	**Fiber** 1g
Fat 9g (sat 4g)	**Cholesterol** 25mg
Protein 7g	**Sodium** 127mg
Carbohydrate 34g	

Exchanges: 1-1/2 starch, 1/2 fruit, 1/2 vegetable, 1/2 lean meat, 1-1/2 fat

Apricot Dessert Soufflé

(Pictured below)

- **3 tablespoons butter**
- **2 tablespoons all-purpose flour**
- **1 cup no-sugar-added apricot pourable fruit***
- **1/3 cup finely chopped dried apricots**
- **3 egg yolks, beaten**
- **4 egg whites**
- **1/4 teaspoon cream of tartar**
- **1/8 teaspoon salt**
- **Fat-free whipped topping (optional)**

*3/4 cup no-sugar-added apricot fruit spread mixed with 1/4 cup warm water can be substituted.

1. Preheat oven to 325°F. Melt butter in medium saucepan. Add flour; cook, stirring constantly, until bubbly.

2. Add pourable fruit and apricots; cook, stirring constantly, about 3 minutes or until thickened. Remove from heat; blend in egg yolks. Cool to room temperature, stirring occasionally.

3. Beat egg whites with cream of tartar and salt in small bowl with electric mixer at high speed until stiff peaks form. Gently fold into apricot mixture. Spoon into 1-1/2-quart soufflé dish. Bake 30 minutes or until puffed and golden brown.** Serve immediately with dollop of whipped topping, if desired.

Makes 6 servings

**Soufflé will be soft in center. For a firmer soufflé, increase baking time to 35 minutes.

Nutrients per Serving: 3/4 cup soufflé

Calories 148	**Fiber** 1g
Fat 9g (sat 5g)	**Cholesterol** 123mg
Protein 4g	**Sodium** 151mg
Carbohydrate 14g	

Exchanges: 1 fruit, 1/2 lean meat, 1-1/2 fat

Apricot Dessert Soufflé

Lemon Cream Peach and Blueberry Pie

(Pictured at right)

3 tablespoons cornstarch

2 cups 1% milk

1/4 cup egg substitute

1/8 teaspoon salt

7 packets sugar substitute*

3 tablespoons lemon juice

1 teaspoon grated lemon peel

1 teaspoon vanilla extract

1 (6-ounce) prepared graham cracker crust

1 cup sliced fresh or thawed frozen peaches

3/4 cup fresh or frozen blueberries, thawed, rinsed and drained

*This recipe was tested with sucralose-based sugar substitute.

1. Combine cornstarch, milk, egg substitute and salt in medium saucepan; whisk until cornstarch is dissolved. Bring to a boil. Cook and stir 2 minutes or until mixture thickens. Stir in sugar substitute, lemon juice, lemon peel and vanilla. Transfer mixture to medium bowl.

2. Place sheet of plastic wrap on top of filling to prevent skin from forming. Let mixture cool to room temperature. Spoon into crust. Decoratively top with peaches and blueberries. Chill completely. Slice into 8 wedges to serve.

Makes 8 servings

Hint: Substitute any of your favorite in-season fruits for the peaches and blueberries.

Nutrients per Serving: 1 pie wedge

Calories 168	**Fiber** 1g
Fat 6g (sat 2g)	**Cholesterol** 3mg
Protein 4g	**Sodium** 200mg
Carbohydrate 25g	

Exchanges: 1 starch, 1/2 fruit, 1/2 milk, 1/2 fat

Sweet as Angels' Kisses

4 egg whites, at room temperature

1/4 teaspoon cream of tartar

1/8 teaspoon salt

1 cup sugar

1/4 teaspoon peppermint or mint extract or desired fruit flavoring

Few drops red or green food coloring

Sprinkles or colored sugar (optional)

1. Preheat oven to 250°F. Line baking sheets with parchment paper or aluminum foil; set aside.

2. Beat egg whites in large bowl with electric mixer at high speed until foamy. Add cream of tartar and salt; beat until soft peaks form. Gradually add sugar, beating until stiff peaks form. Beat in extract and food coloring.

3. Drop rounded tablespoonfuls of egg white mixture onto prepared baking sheets; decorate with sprinkles, if desired.

4. Bake 35 to 45 minutes or until cookies are firm to the touch and just beginning to brown around edges. Remove to wire racks; cool completely.   *Makes 20 servings*

Cocoa Kisses: Omit extract, food coloring and decorations. Beat egg white mixture as directed until stiff peaks form; fold in 1/3 cup unsweetened cocoa powder. Drop rounded tablespoonfuls of egg white mixture onto prepared baking sheets as directed; sprinkle lightly with chocolate sprinkles or finely chopped nuts. Continue as directed.

Nutrients per Serving: 3 meringues

Calories 42	**Fiber** 0g
Fat 0g (sat 0g)	**Cholesterol** 0mg
Protein <1g	**Sodium** 26mg
Carbohydrate 10g	

Exchanges: 1/2 starch

Lemon Cream Peach and Blueberry Pie

Raspberry-Almond Bars

low sodium

(Pictured at right)

2 cups all-purpose flour
1/2 cup EQUAL® SPOONFUL*
1/8 teaspoon salt
8 tablespoons cold margarine or butter, cut into pieces
1 large egg
1 tablespoon fat-free milk or water
2 teaspoons grated lemon peel
2/3 cup seedless raspberry spreadable fruit
1 teaspoon cornstarch
1/2 cup sliced toasted almonds, or walnut or pecan pieces

May substitute 12 packets EQUAL® sweetener.

• Combine flour, Equal® and salt in medium bowl; cut in margarine with pastry blender until mixture resembles coarse crumbs. Mix in egg, milk and lemon peel (mixture will be crumbly).

• Press mixture evenly in bottom of greased 11×7-inch baking dish. Bake in preheated 400°F oven until edges of crust are browned, about 15 minutes. Cool on wire rack.

• Mix spreadable fruit and cornstarch in small saucepan; heat to boiling. Boil until thickened, stirring constantly, 1 minute; cool until warm. Spread mixture evenly over cooled crust; sprinkle with almonds. Bake in preheated 400°F oven until spreadable fruit is thick and bubbly, about 15 minutes. Cool on wire rack; cut into 24 bars. *Makes 24 servings*

Nutrients per Serving: 1 bar

Calories 107	**Fiber** 1g
Fat 5g (sat 1g)	**Cholesterol** 9mg
Protein 2g	**Sodium** 60mg
Carbohydrate 13g	

Exchanges: 1 starch, 1 fat

Eggnog Banana Pie

32 reduced-fat vanilla wafers
3 medium bananas, divided
1/4 teaspoon plus 1/8 teaspoon ground nutmeg, divided
2 cups fat-free milk
1 package (8 ounces) reduced-fat cream cheese
1 package (4-serving size) vanilla sugar-free instant pudding and pie filling mix
1/2 teaspoon brandy extract
1 cup fat-free whipped topping

1. Line bottom and side of 9-inch pie pan with vanilla wafers. Slice 2 bananas and arrange evenly on top of wafers. Sprinkle with 1/4 teaspoon nutmeg; set aside.

2. Place milk, cream cheese, pudding mix and brandy extract in food processor or blender container; process until smooth. Stir in whipped topping.

3. Spoon mixture evenly over bananas; sprinkle with remaining 1/8 teaspoon nutmeg. Cover with plastic wrap and refrigerate until ready to serve (no longer than 4 hours).

4. Just before serving, slice remaining banana and arrange decoratively on top of pie. Slice pie into 8 wedges. *Makes 8 servings*

Nutrients per Serving: 1 pie wedge

Calories 214	**Fiber** 1g
Fat 7g (sat 4g)	**Cholesterol** 14mg
Protein 6g	**Sodium** 297mg
Carbohydrate 33g	

Exchanges: 1-1/2 starch, 1/2 fruit, 1-1/2 fat

Chocolate-Caramel S'Mores

Chocolate-Caramel S'Mores

Quick Recipe   *(Pictured above)*

12 chocolate wafer cookies or chocolate graham cracker squares
2 tablespoons fat-free caramel ice cream topping
6 large marshmallows

1. Prepare coals for grilling. Place 6 wafer cookies top-down on plate. Spread 1 teaspoon caramel topping in center of each wafer to within about 1/4 inch of edge.

2. Spear 1 to 2 marshmallows onto long wood-handled skewer.* Hold several inches above coals 3 to 5 minutes or until marshmallows are golden and very soft, turning slowly. Push 1 marshmallow off into center of caramel. Top with plain wafer. Repeat with remaining marshmallows and wafers.

Makes 6 servings

If skewers don't have protective wood handles, be sure to use oven mitt to protect hand from heat.

Note: In the unlikely event of leftover S'Mores, they can be reheated in the microwave on HIGH 5 to 10 seconds.

Nutrients per Serving: 1 S'More

Calories 72	**Fiber** 0g
Fat 2g (sat 1g)	**Cholesterol** 0mg
Protein 1g	**Sodium** 77mg
Carbohydrate 14g	

Exchanges: 1 starch

☙ ☙ ☙

Oatmeal Almond Balls

Quick Recipe

1/4 cup sliced almonds
2 egg whites
1/3 cup honey
1/2 teaspoon ground cinnamon
1/8 teaspoon salt
1-1/2 cups uncooked quick oats

1. Preheat oven to 350°F. Place almonds on ungreased baking sheet; bake 8 to 10 minutes or until golden brown. Set aside.

2. Combine egg whites, honey, cinnamon and salt in large bowl; stir until well blended. Add oats and toasted almonds; stir until well blended.

3. Drop dough by rounded teaspoonfuls onto ungreased nonstick baking sheets. Bake 12 minutes or until lightly browned. Remove to wire racks; cool completely.

Makes 2 dozen cookies

Nutrients per Serving: 1 cookie

Calories 42	**Fiber** 0g
Fat 1g (sat 0g)	**Cholesterol** 0mg
Protein 1g	**Sodium** 16mg
Carbohydrate 7g	

Exchanges: 1/2 starch

Sugar Cookie Fruit Tart

1 package (18 ounces) refrigerated sugar cookie dough
1 package (8 ounces) fat-free cream cheese
1/4 cup orange marmalade
2 packets sugar substitute *or* equivalent of 4 teaspoons sugar, divided
1 teaspoon vanilla extract
1 can (11 ounces) mandarin oranges, drained
16 fresh strawberries, stemmed and halved
1 kiwifruit, peeled, halved and sliced

1. Preheat oven to 350°F. Coat 12-inch pizza pan with nonstick cooking spray; set aside.

2. Cut dough into 16 slices. Arrange cookie slices 1/2 inch apart on prepared pan. Press dough to cover bottom and sides of pizza pan evenly. Spray fingertips with cooking spray to prevent sticking, if needed. Bake 20 to 22 minutes or until golden brown. Cool completely in pan on wire rack.

3. Beat cream cheese, marmalade, 1 packet sugar substitute and vanilla in medium bowl with electric mixer at high speed until well blended; refrigerate.

4. To assemble, spread cream cheese mixture on top of cooled cookie crust. Mix fruit with remaining packet sugar substitute. Arrange fruit on top of cream cheese mixture. Serve immediately or cover with plastic wrap and refrigerate. Cut into 12 slices before serving.
Makes 12 servings

Nutrients per Serving: 1 tart slice

Calories 265	**Fiber** 2g
Fat 10g (sat 3g)	**Cholesterol** 15mg
Protein 5g	**Sodium** 304mg
Carbohydrate 39g	

Exchanges: 1-1/2 starch, 1 fruit, 2 fat

Hot Fudge Waffle Sundaes

Quick Recipe   *(Pictured below)*

12 frozen mini-waffles
2 tablespoons fat-free sugar-free hot fudge topping
3/4 cup reduced-fat Neapolitan ice cream
4 tablespoons aerosol reduced-fat whipped topping
Colored sprinkles (optional)

1. Heat waffles in toaster until lightly browned. Heat hot fudge topping in microwave according to manufacturer's directions.

2. Arrange 3 waffles on each of 4 serving plates. Top with 1 tablespoon of each ice cream flavor. Evenly drizzle hot fudge topping over top. Top with whipped topping and garnish with sprinkles, if desired. *Makes 4 servings*

Nutrients per Serving: 1 sundae (with 3 mini-waffles)

Calories 157	**Fiber** 1g
Fat 4g (sat 1g)	**Cholesterol** 15mg
Protein 4g	**Sodium** 304mg
Carbohydrate 26g	

Exchanges: 1-1/2 starch, 1 fat

Hot Fudge Waffle Sundae

Peanut Butter & Banana Cookies

Quick Recipe   (Pictured at right)

1/4 cup (1/2 stick) butter, softened
1/2 cup mashed ripe banana (about 1 to 1-1/2 medium)
1/2 cup no-sugar-added natural peanut butter
1/4 cup unsweetened apple juice concentrate
1 egg
1 teaspoon vanilla extract
1 cup all-purpose flour
1/2 teaspoon baking soda
1/4 teaspoon salt
1/2 cup chopped salted peanuts
Whole salted peanuts (optional)

1. Preheat oven to 375°F. Coat cookie sheets with nonstick cooking spray.

2. Beat butter in large bowl until creamy. Add banana and peanut butter; beat until smooth. Blend in apple juice concentrate, egg and vanilla. Beat in flour, baking soda and salt. Stir in chopped peanuts.

3. Drop rounded tablespoonfuls of dough 2 inches apart onto prepared cookie sheets; top each with 1 whole peanut, if desired. Bake 8 minutes or until set. Cool completely on wire racks. Store in tightly covered container.
Makes 2 dozen cookies

Nutrients per Serving: 1 cookie

Calories 100	**Fiber** 1g
Fat 6g (sat 2g)	**Cholesterol** 14mg
Protein 3g	**Sodium** 88mg
Carbohydrate 9g	

Exchanges: 1/2 starch, 1 fat

Rocky Road Pudding

5 tablespoons unsweetened cocoa powder
1/4 cup sugar
3 tablespoons cornstarch
1/8 teaspoon salt
2-1/2 cups 1% milk
2 egg yolks, beaten
2 teaspoons vanilla extract
6 packets sugar substitute *or* equivalent of 1/4 cup sugar
1 cup miniature marshmallows
1/4 cup chopped walnuts, toasted*

*To toast walnuts, spread in single layer on baking sheet. Bake in preheated 350°F oven 8 to 10 minutes or until golden brown, stirring frequently.

1. Combine cocoa, sugar, cornstarch and salt in small saucepan; mix well. Stir in milk until smooth. Cook over medium-high heat, stirring constantly, about 10 minutes or until mixture thickens and begins to boil.

2. Pour about 1/2 cup pudding mixture over beaten egg yolks in small bowl; beat well. Pour mixture back into saucepan. Cook and stir over medium heat an additional 10 minutes or until mixture reaches at least 160°F. Remove from heat; stir in vanilla.

3. Place plastic wrap on surface of pudding. Refrigerate about 20 minutes or until slightly cooled. Remove plastic wrap; stir in sugar substitute. Spoon pudding into 6 dessert dishes; top with marshmallows and nuts. Serve warm or cold.
Makes 6 servings

Nutrients per Serving: 1/3 cup pudding

Calories 190	**Fiber** <1g
Fat 6g (sat 1g)	**Cholesterol** 75mg
Protein 7g	**Sodium** 121mg
Carbohydrate 28g	

Exchanges: 1-1/2 starch, 1/2 milk, 1 fat

Easy Holiday Shortbread Dough

Note: Dough can be stored in the refrigerator up to 2 days, or in the freezer for up to 1 month. Thaw the frozen dough log in the refrigerator overnight before slicing and baking.

Nutrients per Serving: 1 cookie

Calories 106	**Fiber** <1g
Fat 7g (sat 4g)	**Cholesterol** 18mg
Protein <1g	**Sodium** 22mg
Carbohydrate 10g	

Exchanges: 1/2 starch, 1-1/2 fat

Easy Holiday Shortbread Dough

(Pictured above)

1 cup (2 sticks) unsalted butter, softened
1/2 cup powdered sugar
2 tablespoons light brown sugar
1/4 teaspoon salt
2 cups all-purpose flour

1. Beat butter, sugars and salt in large bowl with electric mixer at medium speed until light and fluffy. Add flour, 1/2 cup at a time, beating well after each addition.

2. Form dough into ball; shape into 14-inch log. Wrap log tightly in plastic wrap. Refrigerate 1 hour.

3. Preheat oven to 300°F. Cut log into 1/2-inch-thick slices; place on ungreased cookie sheets. Bake 20 to 25 minutes or until lightly browned. Cool 5 minutes on cookie sheets. Remove to wire racks to cool completely.

Makes 28 cookies

Fruit Kabobs with Mint-Cream Dressing

Quick Recipe

1/2 cup fat-free whipped topping
1 tablespoon minced fresh mint *or*
1/4 teaspoon mint extract
1/2 cup fat-free sour cream
12 (1/2-inch) cantaloupe cubes
12 whole fresh strawberries, stemmed

1. Fold whipped topping and mint into sour cream in small bowl. Divide evenly among 4 small serving bowls; set aside.

2. Alternately thread 3 cantaloupe cubes and 3 strawberries onto each of 4 skewers. Serve with mint-cream dressing for dipping.

Makes 4 servings

Nutrients per Serving: 1 kabob with about 1/4 cup dressing

Calories 70	**Fiber** 1g
Fat 1g (sat <1g)	**Cholesterol** 3mg
Protein 2g	**Sodium** 35mg
Carbohydrate 14g	

Exchanges: 1/2 starch, 1/2 fruit

Hidden Pumpkin Pies

(Pictured at bottom right)

- **1-1/2 cups solid-pack pumpkin**
- **1 cup evaporated fat-free milk**
- **1/2 cup egg substitute *or* 2 eggs**
- **1/4 cup sugar substitute***
- **1-1/4 teaspoons vanilla extract, divided**
- **1 teaspoon pumpkin pie spice****
- **3 egg whites**
- **1/4 teaspoon cream of tartar**
- **1/3 cup honey**

*This recipe was tested with sucralose-based sugar substitute.

**Substitute 1/2 teaspoon ground cinnamon, 1/4 teaspoon ground ginger and 1/8 teaspoon each ground allspice and ground nutmeg for 1 teaspoon pumpkin pie spice, if desired.

1. Preheat oven to 350°F.

2. Combine pumpkin, evaporated milk, egg substitute, sugar substitute, 1 teaspoon vanilla and pumpkin pie spice in large bowl. Pour into 6 (6-ounce) custard cups or 6 (3/4-cup) soufflé dishes. Place in shallow baking dish or pan. Pour boiling water around custard cups to depth of 1 inch. Bake 25 minutes.

3. Meanwhile, beat egg whites, cream of tartar and remaining 1/4 teaspoon vanilla in large bowl with electric mixer at high speed until soft peaks form. Gradually add honey, beating until stiff peaks form.

4. Spread egg white mixture over top of hot pumpkin pies. Return to oven. Bake 15 to 16 minutes or until tops of pies are golden brown. Remove from oven. Let stand 10 minutes. Serve warm.   *Makes 6 servings*

Nutrients per Serving: 1 pie

Calories 148	**Fiber** 2g
Fat 2g (sat 1g)	**Cholesterol** 54mg
Protein 8g	**Sodium** 133mg
Carbohydrate 27g	

Exchanges: 2 starch, 1/2 lean meat

Fruit & Cheese Crisps

Quick Recipe

- **1/2 cup part-skim ricotta cheese**
- **1 tablespoon thawed frozen unsweetened apple juice concentrate plus 1/4 teaspoon almond extract**
- **1/4 cup slivered almonds, toasted***
- **4 no-sugar-added crispbread or crackerbread rectangles,** any flavor**
- **1/4 cup sliced fresh strawberries**
- **1/4 cup sliced fresh peaches**
- **No-sugar-added strawberry or raspberry pourable fruit (optional)**

*To toast almonds, spread in single layer on baking sheet. Bake in preheated 350°F oven 8 to 10 minutes or until golden brown, stirring frequently.

Combine ricotta cheese and liqueur; mix well. Stir in almonds; spread evenly over crispbread. Top with fruit. Brush with pourable fruit, if desired. Serve immediately.

Makes 4 servings

Nutrients per Serving: 1 crisp rectangle

Calories 139	**Fiber** 3g
Fat 6g (sat 2g)	**Cholesterol** 9mg
Protein 6g	**Sodium** 65mg
Carbohydrate 14g	

Exchanges: 1 starch, 1/2 lean meat, 1 fat

Hidden Pumpkin Pie

Cinnamon Dessert Tacos with Fruit Salsa

Quick Recipe   (Pictured at right)

> **1 cup sliced fresh strawberries**
> **1 cup diced fresh pineapple**
> **1 cup diced peeled kiwifruit**
> **1/2 teaspoon minced jalapeño pepper***
>   **(optional)**
> **2 packets sugar substitute** *or* **equivalent of**
>   **4 teaspoons sugar (optional)**
> **3 tablespoons sugar**
> **1 tablespoon ground cinnamon**
> **6 (8-inch) flour tortillas**
>   **Nonstick cooking spray**

*Jalapeño peppers can sting and irritate the skin, so wear rubber gloves when handling peppers and do not touch your eyes.

1. Stir together strawberries, pineapple, kiwifruit and jalapeño pepper and sugar substitute, if desired, in large bowl; set aside. Combine sugar and cinnamon in small bowl; set aside.

2. Spray tortilla lightly on both sides with cooking spray. Heat over medium heat in nonstick skillet until slightly puffed and golden brown. Remove from heat; immediately dust both sides with sugar-cinnamon mixture. Shake excess sugar-cinnamon back into small bowl. Repeat cooking and dusting process with remaining tortillas.

3. Fold tortillas in half and fill with fruit mixture. Serve immediately.   *Makes 6 servings*

Nutrients per Serving: 1 taco (with 1/2 cup salsa)

Calories 183	**Fiber** 4g
Fat 3g (sat <1g)	**Cholesterol** 0mg
Protein 4g	**Sodium** 169mg
Carbohydrate 36g	

Exchanges: 1-1/2 starch, 1 fruit, 1/2 fat

Sugar Cookies

> **1-3/4 cups all-purpose flour**
> **1/4 cup unprocessed bran**
> **1/2 teaspoon baking soda**
> **1/8 teaspoon salt**
> **1/2 cup (1 stick) soft baking butter with**
>   **canola oil**
> **1/4 cup sugar**
> **1/4 cup unsweetened applesauce**
> **1 egg white**
> **1 teaspoon vanilla extract**
> **2 tablespoons plus 1/2 teaspoon red or**
>   **green fine decorating sugar**

1. Combine flour, bran, baking soda and salt in medium bowl; set aside.

2. Beat butter and sugar in large bowl with electric mixer at medium speed 1 minute or until creamy. Add applesauce, egg white and vanilla. Beat on low speed until just blended. Increase speed to medium; beat until smooth.

3. Gradually add flour mixture to butter mixture, beating on low speed until well blended. Divide dough into 2 equal portions. Roll each portion into 11-inch log. Wrap in plastic wrap. Freeze at least 1 hour.

4. Preheat oven to 350°F. Remove logs from freezer. Cut widthwise into 1/4-inch-thick slices, turning log slightly after each slice to maintain round shape.

5. Dip half of 1 side of each cookie into decorating sugar. Place cookies, sugar side up, on cookie sheets. Bake 6 to 8 minutes or until set. Cool on cookie sheets 2 minutes. Remove to wire racks to cool completely.

Makes 68 cookies

Nutrients per Serving: 2 cookies

Calories 60	**Fiber** <1g
Fat 4g (sat 1g)	**Cholesterol** 6mg
Protein <1g	**Sodium** 66mg
Carbohydrate 8g	

Exchanges: 1/2 starch

Cinnamon Dessert Taco with Fruit Salsa

Christmas Mouse Ice Cream

Christmas Mouse Ice Creams

(Pictured above)

2 cups no-sugar-added fat-free vanilla ice cream
1 package (4 ounces) single-serving graham cracker crusts
6 sugar-free chocolate sandwich cookies, separated and cream filling removed
12 black sugar-free jelly beans
6 red sugar-free jelly beans
36 chocolate sprinkles (approximately 1/4 teaspoon)

1. Place 1 rounded scoop (about 1/3 cup) ice cream into each crust. Freeze 10 minutes.

2. Press 2 cookie halves into each ice cream scoop for ears. Decorate as shown in above photo. Freeze 10 minutes before serving.
Makes 6 servings

Nutrients per Serving: 1 ice cream dessert

Calories 219	**Fiber** 1g
Fat 8g (sat 1g)	**Cholesterol** 0mg
Protein 4g	**Sodium** 209mg
Carbohydrate 35g	

Exchanges: 2-1/2 starch, 1 fat

Ginger-Spiced Pumpkin Pie

1 cup finely crushed gingersnap cookies
1/4 cup (1/2 stick) butter, melted
2 egg whites
3/4 cup packed light brown sugar
1 can (15 ounces) solid-pack pumpkin
1 cup evaporated fat-free milk
1 teaspoon ground ginger
1 teaspoon ground cinnamon
1 teaspoon vanilla extract
1/2 teaspoon salt

1. Combine crushed cookies and butter in medium bowl; mix well. Press onto bottom and up side of 9-inch glass pie plate. Refrigerate 30 minutes.

2. Preheat oven to 350°F.

3. Beat egg whites and brown sugar in large bowl. Add pumpkin, evaporated milk, ginger, cinnamon, vanilla and salt; mix well. Pour into crust.

4. Bake 60 to 70 minutes or until center is set. Transfer pie to wire rack; cool 30 minutes. Serve warm or at room temperature. Cut into 8 wedges to serve.
Makes 8 servings

Nutrients per Serving: 1 pie wedge

Calories 234	**Fiber** 2g
Fat 8g (sat 4g)	**Cholesterol** 18mg
Protein 5g	**Sodium** 365mg
Carbohydrate 38g	

Exchanges: 2-1/2 starch, 1 fat

Tip

Evaporated milk is canned, unsweetened milk with 60% of the water removed. The only difference between this and sweetened condensed milk is the absence of sugar. When slightly frozen, evaporated milk can be beaten to make a low-cost whipped cream substitute.

Grilled Banana Split

Quick Recipe (Pictured on page 150)

1 large firm ripe banana
1/2 teaspoon butter, melted
2 tablespoons fat-free chocolate syrup
1/2 teaspoon orange liqueur (optional)
2/3 cup no-sugar-added fat-free vanilla ice cream
2 tablespoons sliced almonds, toasted*

*To toast almonds, spread in single layer on baking sheet. Bake in preheated 350°F oven 8 to 10 minutes or until golden brown, stirring frequently.

1. Prepare grill for direct grilling.

2. Cut unpeeled banana in half lengthwise; brush melted butter over cut sides. Grill banana, cut side down, over medium-hot coals 2 minutes or until lightly browned; turn. Grill 2 minutes more or until tender.

3. Combine syrup and liqueur, if desired, in small bowl.

4. Cut banana in half widthwise; carefully remove peel. Place 2 pieces banana in each of 2 serving bowls; top both with 1/3 cup ice cream, 1 tablespoon chocolate syrup and 1 tablespoon almonds; serve immediately.

Makes 2 servings

Nutrients per Serving: 1 Grilled Banana Split

Calories 198 **Fiber** 2g
Fat 5g (sat 1g) **Cholesterol** 3mg
Protein 5g **Sodium** 59mg
Carbohydrate 33g

Exchanges: 1 starch, 1 fruit, 1 fat

PM Snack Bars

(Pictured below)

3 tablespoons creamy peanut butter
2 tablespoons molasses
2 egg whites
2 tablespoons ground flaxseed
4 cups crisp rice cereal
1/2 cup sliced almonds
1 ounce bittersweet chocolate, melted

1. Preheat oven to 350°F. Place peanut butter in small microwave-safe bowl. Microwave on LOW (30%) 30 seconds or until peanut butter is melted. Stir in molasses; cool.

2. Place egg whites and flaxseed in blender container. Blend until foamy. Pour into large bowl. Add peanut butter mixture; stir until smooth. Stir in cereal and almonds; stir until cereal is evenly coated.

3. Spray 9-inch square baking pan with nonstick cooking spray. Press cereal mixture into pan. Bake 20 to 25 minutes or until browned on top. Cool completely in pan on wire rack. Cut into 16 bars. Drizzle melted chocolate over bars.

Makes 16 servings

Nutrients per Serving: 1 (2-1/4-inch) square bar

Calories 91 **Fiber** 1g
Fat 4g (sat 1g) **Cholesterol** <1mg
Protein 3g **Sodium** 24mg
Carbohydrate 11g

Exchanges: 1/2 starch, 1 fat

PM Snack Bars

Apple Cranberry Streusel Pie

(Pictured at right)

Pastry for single crust 9-inch pie
1 cup EQUAL® SPOONFUL*
1 tablespoon cornstarch
1-1/2 cups fresh or thawed frozen cranberries
1 cup apple cider or unsweetened juice
1/4 cup EQUAL® SPOONFUL**
3/4 teaspoon ground cinnamon
1/4 teaspoon *each* salt and ground nutmeg
5 cups sliced, peeled Granny Smith or other baking apples (about 5 medium)
Streusel Topping (recipe follows)

*May substitute 24 packets EQUAL® sweetener.

**May substitute 6 packets EQUAL® sweetener.

• Roll pastry on floured surface into circle 1 inch larger than inverted 9-inch pie plate. Ease pastry into plate; trim and flute edge. Set aside.

• Combine 1 cup Equal® and cornstarch in small saucepan; stir in cranberries and apple cider. Heat to boiling. Reduce heat and simmer, stirring constantly, until thickened, about 1 minute.

• Combine 1/4 cup Equal®, cinnamon, salt and nutmeg; sprinkle over apples in large bowl. Toss to coat. Pour cranberry mixture over apples and mix gently. Arrange fruit in pie pastry; sprinkle Streusel Topping over fruit.

• Bake in preheated 400°F oven 50 to 60 minutes or until pastry is golden and apples are tender. Cover loosely with foil during last 20 to 30 minutes if browning too quickly. Serve warm or at room temperature.   *Makes 8 servings*

Streusel Topping

1/4 cup uncooked quick or old-fashioned oats
3 tablespoons all-purpose flour
1/2 cup EQUAL® SPOONFUL*
1 teaspoon ground cinnamon
1/2 teaspoon ground nutmeg
4 tablespoons cold stick butter, in pieces

*May substitute 12 packets EQUAL® sweetener.

• Combine oats, flour, 1/2 cup Equal®, cinnamon and nutmeg in small bowl. Cut in butter with pastry blender until mixture resembles coarse crumbs. Sprinkle over fruit in pie pastry.

Nutrients per Serving: 1 pie wedge

Calories 238	**Fiber** 2g
Fat 11g (sat 4g)	**Cholesterol** 5mg
Protein 2g	**Sodium** 201mg
Carbohydrate 35g	

Exchanges: 1 starch, 1-1/2 fruit, 2 fat

Cream Cheese Brownie Royale

1 package (about 15 ounces) reduced-fat brownie mix
2/3 cup cold coffee or water
1 package (8 ounces) reduced-fat cream cheese
1/4 cup fat-free milk
5 packets sugar substitute *or* equivalent of 3 tablespoons plus 1 teaspoon sugar
1/2 teaspoon vanilla extract

1. Preheat oven to 350°F. Coat 13×9-inch baking pan with nonstick cooking spray. Combine brownie mix and coffee in large bowl. Pour into prepared pan.

2. Beat remaining ingredients in medium bowl with electric mixer at medium speed until smooth. Spoon, in dollops, over brownie mixture. Swirl into brownie mixture with tip of knife. Bake 30 to 35 minutes or until toothpick inserted into center comes out clean. Cool completely in pan on wire rack. Cover with foil; refrigerate 8 hours or until ready to serve. Cut into 16 squares.   *Makes 16 servings*

Nutrients per Serving: 1 brownie square

Calories 167	**Fiber** 1g
Fat 5g (sat 2g)	**Cholesterol** 7mg
Protein 4g	**Sodium** 181mg
Carbohydrate 28g	

Exchanges: 2 starch, 1/2 fat

Apple Cranberry Streusel Pie

Waist-Watcher's Cocoa Dessert

Waist-Watcher's Cocoa Dessert

(Pictured above)

1 envelope unflavored gelatin
1-3/4 cups cold water
2/3 cup nonfat dry milk powder
2 egg yolks, slightly beaten
3 tablespoons HERSHEY'S Cocoa
1/4 teaspoon salt
1/2 cup sugar or equivalent amount of granulated sugar substitute
2 teaspoons vanilla extract
1/2 cup thawed frozen light non-dairy whipped topping
Assorted fresh fruit, cut up (optional)
Additional frozen light non-dairy whipped topping, thawed (optional)
Additional HERSHEY'S Cocoa (optional)

1. Sprinkle gelatin over water in medium saucepan; let stand 5 minutes to soften. Add milk powder, egg yolks, 3 tablespoons cocoa and salt. Cook over medium heat, stirring constantly, until mixture begins to boil; remove from heat. Stir in sugar and vanilla. Pour mixture into large bowl. Refrigerate, stirring occasionally, until mixture mounds slightly when dropped from spoon, about 1 hour.

2. Fold 1/2 cup whipped topping into chocolate mixture. Pour into 6 individual dessert dishes. Cover; refrigerate until firm, about 4 hours. Garnish individual dessert dishes with assorted fresh fruit or additional whipped topping, sprinkled with additional cocoa, if desired.

Makes 6 servings

Note: A 3-cup mold may be used in place of individual dessert dishes, if desired.

Nutrients per Serving: about 1/2 cup dessert

Calories 93	**Fiber** 1g
Fat 3g (sat 1g)	**Cholesterol** 72mg
Protein 5g	**Sodium** 144mg
Carbohydrate 11g	

Exchanges: 1 milk, 1/2 fat

‰ ‰ ‰

Orange Smoothies

Quick Recipe

1 cup fat-free vanilla ice cream
3/4 cup 1% milk
1/4 cup orange juice concentrate

1. Combine ice cream, milk and orange juice concentrate in food processor or blender container; process until smooth.

2. Pour mixture into 2 glasses; garnish as desired. Serve immediately.

Makes 2 servings

Nutrients per Serving: 1 smoothie (1/2 of total recipe)

Calories 185	**Fiber** <1g
Fat 1g (sat <1g)	**Cholesterol** 4mg
Protein 8g	**Sodium** 117mg
Carbohydrate 38g	

Exchanges: 1 starch, 1 fruit, 1/2 milk

Reduced-Sugar Chocolate Chocolate Chip Cookies

low sodium

1/2 cup (1 stick) butter or margarine, softened
1/4 cup granulated sugar
1/2 cup measure-for-measure sugar substitute
1 egg
1 teaspoon vanilla extract
1 cup all-purpose flour
3 tablespoons HERSHEY'S Cocoa or HERSHEY'S SPECIAL DARK® Cocoa
1/2 teaspoon baking soda
1/8 teaspoon salt
2 tablespoons skim milk
1/3 cup HERSHEY'S MINI CHIPS™ Semi-Sweet Chocolate Chips

1. Heat oven to 375°F.

2. Beat butter, granulated sugar and sugar substitute with electric mixer on medium speed in medium bowl until well blended. Add egg and vanilla; beat well. Stir together flour, cocoa, baking soda and salt; add alternately with milk to butter mixture, beating until well blended. Stir in small chocolate chips. Drop by teaspoons onto ungreased cookie sheet.

3. Bake 7 to 9 minutes or just until set. Remove to wire rack and cool completely.

Makes 3 dozen cookies

Nutrients per Serving: 2 cookies

Calories 107	**Fiber** 1g
Fat 6g (sat 4g)	**Cholesterol** 25mg
Protein 2g	**Sodium** 57mg
Carbohydrate 11g	

Exchanges: 1 starch, 1 fat

Cheese-Filled Poached Pears

low sodium

(Pictured on page 150)

1-1/2 quarts cranberry-raspberry juice cocktail
2 ripe Bartlett pears with stems, peeled
2 tablespoons reduced-fat cream cheese
2 teaspoons crumbled Gorgonzola cheese
1 tablespoon chopped walnuts

1. Bring juice to a boil in medium saucepan over high heat. Add pears; reduce heat to medium-low. Simmer 15 minutes or until pears are tender, turning occasionally.

2. Remove pears from saucepan; discard liquid. Let pears stand 10 minutes or until cool enough to handle.

3. Combine cheeses in small bowl until well blended. Cut thin slice off bottom of each pear so pears stand evenly. Cut pears lengthwise in half, leaving stems intact. Scoop out seeds and membranes to form small hole inside each pear half. Fill holes with cheese mixture. Press halves together.

4. Place nuts in large bowl. Roll pears in nuts to coat. Cover; refrigerate until ready to serve.

Makes 2 servings

Nutrients per Serving: 1 filled pear

Calories 240	**Fiber** 4g
Fat 7g (sat 3g)	**Cholesterol** 13mg
Protein 4g	**Sodium** 98mg
Carbohydrate 45g	

Exchanges: 3 fruit, 1/2 lean meat, 1 fat

Strawberry Trifle

Strawberry Trifle

Quick Recipe

    1/4 cup sugar
    3 tablespoons cornstarch
1-1/2 cups fat-free half-and-half
    1/3 cup egg substitute
    2 tablespoons reduced-fat sour cream
    2 teaspoons vanilla extract
2-3/4 cups sliced fresh strawberries, divided
    1 tablespoon orange juice or Marsala wine
    1 can (15 ounces) mandarin orange segments, drained
    1 can (11 ounces) mandarin orange segments, drained
    1 large banana, peeled and thinly sliced
1-1/2 teaspoons lemon juice
    1 prepared (10-ounce) angel food cake, cut into 1-inch cubes

1. Blend sugar, cornstarch and half-and-half together in small saucepan. Bring to a boil over medium heat, stirring constantly. Boil 1 minute or until mixture thickens, stirring constantly. Reduce heat to medium-low.

2. Blend 1/3 cup hot half-and-half mixture into egg substitute in small bowl. Stir into remaining half-and-half mixture. Cook 2 minutes, stirring constantly. Remove from heat. Let stand 10 minutes, stirring frequently. Stir in sour cream and vanilla.

3. Place 3/4 cup strawberries and orange juice in blender or food processor container; purée until smooth. Reserve 15 orange segments and 1/4 cup strawberries in small bowl. Combine banana, remaining 1-3/4 cups strawberries, remaining orange segments and lemon juice in medium bowl.

4. Place half of cake cubes in bottom of 2- to 3-quart trifle dish or straight-sided glass serving bowl. Drizzle half of strawberry purée over cake. Top with half of fruit mixture and half of custard. Repeat layers with remaining cake, strawberry purée, fruit mixture and custard.

5. Arrange 15 reserved orange segments and 1/4 cup reserved strawberries decoratively over final custard layer on triple top.

Makes 12 servings

Nutrients per Serving: about 1 cup trifle

Calories 160	**Fiber** 1g
Fat 1g (sat <1g)	**Cholesterol** 1mg
Protein 4g	**Sodium** 222mg
Carbohydrate 34g	

Exchanges: 1-1/2 starch, 1 fruit

Tip

Bananas can be frozen if they are left whole and in their peels. Wrap them airtight and freeze them for up to 6 months. If the banana was not overripe when it was frozen, it can be sliced while still frozen.

Acknowledgments

*The publisher would like to thank the companies and organizations
listed below for the use of their recipes and photographs
in this publication.*

ACH Food Companies, Inc.

California Dried Plum Board

California Olive Industry

Cherry Marketing Institute

Del Monte Corporation

Equal® sweetener

The Hershey Company

Jennie-O Turkey Store®

Kashi® Company

The Kingsford® Products Co.

Minnesota Cultivated Wild Rice Council

Mott's® is a registered trademark of Mott's, LLP

Mrs. Dash®

National Watermelon Promotion Board

The Quaker® Oatmeal Kitchens

Riviana Foods Inc.

US Dry Bean Council

USA Rice Federation™

Walnut Marketing Board

General Index

Index **185**

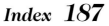

188 Index

Icon Index

METRIC CONVERSION CHART

VOLUME MEASUREMENTS (dry)

1/8 teaspoon = 0.5 mL
1/4 teaspoon = 1 mL
1/2 teaspoon = 2 mL
3/4 teaspoon = 4 mL
1 teaspoon = 5 mL
1 tablespoon = 15 mL
2 tablespoons = 30 mL
1/4 cup = 60 mL
1/3 cup = 75 mL
1/2 cup = 125 mL
2/3 cup = 150 mL
3/4 cup = 175 mL
1 cup = 250 mL
2 cups = 1 pint = 500 mL
3 cups = 750 mL
4 cups = 1 quart = 1 L

VOLUME MEASUREMENTS (fluid)

1 fluid ounce (2 tablespoons) = 30 mL
4 fluid ounces (1/2 cup) = 125 mL
8 fluid ounces (1 cup) = 250 mL
12 fluid ounces (1 1/2 cups) = 375 mL
16 fluid ounces (2 cups) = 500 mL

WEIGHTS (mass)

1/2 ounce = 15 g
1 ounce = 30 g
3 ounces = 90 g
4 ounces = 120 g
8 ounces = 225 g
10 ounces = 285 g
12 ounces = 360 g
16 ounces = 1 pound = 450 g

DIMENSIONS

1/16 inch = 2 mm
1/8 inch = 3 mm
1/4 inch = 6 mm
1/2 inch = 1.5 cm
3/4 inch = 2 cm
1 inch = 2.5 cm

OVEN TEMPERATURES

250°F = 120°C
275°F = 140°C
300°F = 150°C
325°F = 160°C
350°F = 180°C
375°F = 190°C
400°F = 200°C
425°F = 220°C
450°F = 230°C

BAKING PAN SIZES

Utensil	Size in Inches/Quarts	Metric Volume	Size in Centimeters
Baking or Cake Pan (square or rectangular)	8×8×2	2 L	20×20×5
	9×9×2	2.5 L	23×23×5
	12×8×2	3 L	30×20×5
	13×9×2	3.5 L	33×23×5
Loaf Pan	8×4×3	1.5 L	20×10×7
	9×5×3	2 L	23×13×7
Round Layer Cake Pan	8×1½	1.2 L	20×4
	9×1½	1.5 L	23×4
Pie Plate	8×1¼	750 mL	20×3
	9×1¼	1 L	23×3
Baking Dish or Casserole	1 quart	1 L	—
	1½ quart	1.5 L	—
	2 quart	2 L	—